The Acceptance Guidebook

Spiritual Solutions for Active Minds

Todd Schaefer

The Acceptance Guidebook:
Spiritual Solutions for Active Minds

By Todd Schaefer

As You Wish Publishing Phoenix, Arizona

First Edition, 2011

Second Edition, 2021

ISBN 13 - 978-1-951131-30-2

Published in the United States of America

For more information, visit the publisher's website at:
www.asyouwishpublishing.com.

Praise for *The Acceptance Guidebook*

"Todd Schaefer is the best kind of spiritual teacher. He doesn't tell us what to do or how to do it. Instead, with at times touching vulnerability, he reminds us of our inherent value, empowers us to surrender to the greater wisdom of our innate divinity and guides us on the only journey that matters: toward accepting all of who we are. A profound and enriching book."

— **Mark David Gerson,** inspirational speaker, author/screenwriter *The MoonQuest* and *The Voice of the Muse: Answering the Call to Write*

"Todd Schaefer offers brilliant insights into the nature of the human mind-labyrinth. The Acceptance Guidebook lights a lantern that helps the reader to walk the labyrinth without endlessly bumping into walls."

— **Tom Von Deck,** Corporate Meditation Trainer, speaker and author of *Oceanic Mind – The Deeper Meditation Training Course*

"Todd's journey is an inspiring testament to the divine power of 'letting go and letting God.' The Acceptance Guidebook is a work of art, blessing the reader with deep spiritual meaning through seemingly simplistic language. This book is jam-packed with transformational insights and stories, encompassing prayer, relationships, surrender, forgiveness, and much more in between.

Each time I open it for a read, whether things in life are good, bad, or merely okay, I am graced with an inevitable sense of contentment...an authentic presence of peace."

— **Nathan Anderson,** author of *A Good Dose of God: Everybody'sBest Friend*

"Even the guided need guiding. This book appeals to all levels of spirituality and expounds on what it truly means to be human; in all aspects of compassion, success and wisdom. Todd effectively and harmoniously splits the 'black' and 'white' of our belief system and raises the 'gray' to a heightened level of awareness and acceptance. Todd's pearls of wisdom have helped me fulfill many of my personal goals in overcoming anxiety and fears that I thought would carry on for decades. A must-read for anyone and everyone wanting to live a full, happy and complete life!"

— **Jennifer L. Fox,** B.A. English Literature, Colby-Sawyer College, *Greenfield, NH*

"The Acceptance Guidebook walks us through the shift from a journey of unconscious living into a life of awareness. Todd offers complex spiritual ideas that are simple to read and understand, making them easy to apply to our lives. His gentle teachings, personal observations and stories have created a book that carries the intentions of a true teacher."

— **Julieanne Paige,** founder, *Be Inspired Today*

"Todd Schaefer is definitely "on the path" and, for my money, has "chosen the better part." He has seen that the surrender to the goodness intrinsic to a Divine Source and then emulating that source is key to any success which follows that acceptance. Todd's keen ability for deep thinking and objective observation will lead you into your own insights as it did him. Todd's writing is a solid contribution toward the unfoldment of more good here on earth because it lauds individuality."

— **Pat Matson,** teacher, *The Walter Method*

"Todd Schaefer has gifted the world with a book and knowledge that shows us a path to true empowerment. Acceptance of where we are in each moment is how we truly transcend to the next moment and then to the one after that and ultimately to exist in a place of inner peace. Todd's message is for teachers and students, for healers and those who wish to be healed. It is something that rings true for everyone who is walking a spiritual path of awakening."

—**Tricia Baehr,** co-founder, *Sweet Water Sustainability Institute, Knoxville, TN*

"The Acceptance Guidebook is one of the most human books I've ever read. When reading, I felt as if I was talking not only to a live person but to my inner self. Completely comprehensible, the text offers a journey through our relationship with ourselves and the world, creating a kinder, more compassionately observant you.

Whether it's judgment, fear or social conditioning, this book will become a companion in guiding you into surrender, trust, and conscious awareness."

— **Bryn Cartwright,** Yoga teacher, Sound Therapist, *CA*

"Todd really gets to the essence of the matter of acceptance. He gives you tools and techniques to make it happen and inspires you to get in touch with the spiritual nature of your own self-acceptance. A great read for anyone on the path of self-transformation."

— **Nicky Highlen,** Owner and Chief Inspiration Officer of *Your Infinite Potential, LLC, Metamora, MI*

"Relationships, surrender, forgiveness, acceptance – just four of many outstanding topics in Todd's inspiring new book. I found his personal experiences of living from the heart instead of his identity very moving. It takes tremendous courage to be truly authentic, to realize that everything we are looking for is already within us. We are our own gurus. A wonderful traveling companion and road map for anyone's journey and a great tool for those seeking self- awareness, as well as fun, practical guidance on ways we can all live a more magical life."

— **Gina Baksa,** writer, Spirituality in Business Coach, *London, UK*

"Todd writes an enlightening and inspirational book, writing of his own personal spiritual journey and

experience as a spiritual teacher. He encourages us to look beyond our own ego and its limitations to find our own truth, empowering us that we are more than just the sum of our own ego and reminding us that we are spiritual beings on a human journey. His book gives insight into how to embrace God within us and to experience humanity more positively, and get much more out of the human experience which we experience day to day. The Acceptance Guidebook is an invaluable resource however far you may be on your spiritual journey."

— **Steven Hardman,** founder, *Global Spiritual Awakening Network*

"Todd Schaefer has created a nuanced, no-nonsense series of lessons specifically intended for the restless spiritual seeker. He understands the value of meeting the reader at his or her readiness level without compromising the potential impact of the message, which is quite a trick. The Acceptance Guidebook often feels more like an on-demand spiritual coach than a book, which should speak volumes for its universal applicability. Highly recommended for anyone ready and willing to fully embrace and accept themselves as they move forward on their personal pathway, regardless of where they perceive themselves to be because acceptance is the key!"

— **Kenny Jaworski,** pianist, composer, *St. Louis, MO*

For Katherine

"We tend to develop abilities to make ourselves valuable, and later we come to find that those things aren't what make us valuable."

— **Todd Schaefer**

CONTENTS

Foreword

With today's technology, we can instantly meet people around the globe or stay abreast with friends, sometimes hundreds at a time. We can touch countless lives without ever knowing we touched them. We can create entire communities of like-minded people. In this sense, the world has drastically shrunk. Sharing our thoughts with others is only an instantaneous click of a button away. Yet, in the same sense, our technology has vastly enlarged our world because it allows us to broaden and raise our consciousness as others touch our hearts and minds. Our realms of understanding expand, sometimes when least expected. With every increase of awareness, we gain more insight, and with our every gain, the world grows too.

I experienced this concurrent shrinking of the world and expansion of consciousness in 2005 when I met Todd Schaefer via the Internet. I stumbled upon a group of like-minded people who gathered at what I affectionately called "a watering hole of spirituality." It was where I turned to feed my spiritual hunger. People as far from each other as New Zealand, Australia, China, India, Russia, Spain, Germany, and the Netherlands (to name a few), and in cultures as diverse as the oceans and global separation could make us, came together to share a commonality — our quest for enlightenment and spiritual growth. Todd spearheaded the group.

As we shared more of our beliefs and feelings, my friendship and trust in Todd grew and included marathon telephone conversations during which we shared our struggles and triumphs. I'd talk to him about my frustrations until he'd say a key word or phrase and resolve a seemingly insurmountable tangle of conflicts. Never did the resolution come from being told what to do or how to do it, but rather through his recognition of my spiritual connectivity to God.

Later, I had an occasion to spend time with Todd when he invited me to his fiancé's birthday party. Since I came from quite a distance out of town, I spent the weekend at their home. From the moment of my arrival and throughout the entire weekend, whether in quiet company with only the two of them or surrounded by friends and family, I felt like their guest of honor.

I puzzled over the feeling until I realized Todd honored every guest, just as he honors everyone by recognizing and accepting their Divinity. Todd's acceptance of another's spirituality isn't something that develops as he gets to know them; it's permanently inherent in every facet of his association with humanity, and it is evidenced time and again throughout his book *The Acceptance Guidebook: Spiritual Solutions for Active Minds*. His acceptance is the basis on which he wrote the book, and by sharing it, he recognizes and honors your Divinity too. Absolutely. In this inspiring, growth-enhancing book, Todd shrinks the world by divinely connecting each of us while, at the same time, he enlarges the world by expanding our consciousness.

Ronnie (Rhonda) Carroll, Published Author

World-Wide published poet Philosopher

Acknowledgments

I thank each person who has stepped into my life and has given me the grace of their presence and teachings. Each person has somehow contributed to the creation of this book by being a positive influence for me. Everyone has unique gifts and talents to share, and I am touched that I have been able to receive what each person has offered. Although there are too many to mention, I thank the following members of my family and friends. Each has exhibited great commitment to service, love and acceptance while still allowing him or herself to be human. For your support, I send my heartfelt thanks to my wife, Kyra Schaefer, parents Gary Schaefer, Mary Schaefer, and Phyllis Schaefer, ministers Reverend Patricia Jordan, Reverend Joseph Lahue, Tomasita Lahue and Simon. Thank you to Kenny Jaworski for your many years of close friendship and support. Thank you to Jo Lynda Manion for your editing and proofreading. Thank you to Keidi Keating for marketing the book with your incisive words. Thank you to Ronnie Carroll, Natasha Cannon, Julieanne Paige, Leslie Smith, Lyn Gallant, Nathan Anderson, Shauna Belli, Stephanie Flaiz and Maureen Cowan for your years of friendship and support. Thank you to the Crimson Circle, Abraham-Hicks, my angel team, God, the Lord Jesus Christ and the Holy Spirit. Thank you also to everyone at As You Wish Publishing who has helped in the production of this book.

Disclaimer

The materials in this book are provided for informational purposes only and should not be relied on for medical, legal, psychiatric, or any other professional advice of any nature. If legal or other expert assistance is required, the services of a competent professional should be sought.

Every effort has been made to make this book as helpful and as accurate as possible; however, there may be typographical and content mistakes. Therefore, this text should be used only as a general guide and not as an ultimate resource.

The material in this book is provided "as is" and without warranties of any kind, either expressed or implied. The publisher and author do not warrant or make representations regarding the use or the results of applying the ideas within this book in terms of their correctness, accuracy, reliability or otherwise.

The purpose of this book is to educate. The author and As You Wish Publishing shall have neither liability nor responsibility to any person or entity with respect to any loss or damage caused or alleged to have been caused, directly or indirectly, by the information contained in this book.

Introduction by the Author

This book was written between 2005 and 2010 and was originally published in 2011. While the first edition is out of print and no longer available through the original publisher, it has been republished as a second edition in 2021.

My Non-Acceptance

If you had asked me six years ago (in 2005) why I wrote this book, I would not have been able to answer that its purpose was for me to learn acceptance. Instead, I would have said that its purpose was for me to find answers. I did not yet know that my need to find answers would change when I felt acceptance.

Let me be the first to tell you that I am not a perfect example of someone who accepts everything without exception. That is why this can only be a guidebook and not a rulebook. I have my unique share of things that I have not yet accepted about myself and my life.

Today, I gratefully understand that the things I need to accept serve as my clay. Without them, I wouldn't know where to mold or how to sculpt myself.

My History

Since before I can remember, I have been intrigued with the functioning of my mind and spirit. I always wanted to know more, to understand, to figure it all out. Somehow, I seemed to believe that if I understood how my mind functioned spiritually, it would be the best approach to my path of self-discovery. In thirty-two years on this earth, this desire to experience, express and expand has not diminished.

My upbringing was pretty normal: a functional, middle-class Midwestern family. Most of the time, I was a good kid, didn't cause trouble except for occasionally challenging authority. I'd speak up if I thought my way of doing things was more efficient. I had a curious, analytical and intuitive mind. Sounds like your normal adolescent teenager, right? I was friendly and compassionate while having my pubescent quirks. But it wasn't until my lateteens that I began making more interesting discoveries about who I was.

When I was about 17 years old, I had noticed anxiety was beginning to play a dominant role in my life experience. I didn't know why. Maybe school pressures to perform well. My parents didn't push me to high performance – I pushed myself.

I suffered fears and wondered where they came from. I dug into my memories. Perhaps I'd stumble onto an anxious third-grade experience that was just now resurfacing. Perhaps the trouble was biological, an imprint from my parents. Maybe the trouble was in my psychological makeup. Whatever it was, I felt compelled to learn more about it. It was my initiation.

I spoke with my dad about the anxieties. He recommended his self-help and affirmation books. These helped a great deal because they guided me to focus my attention. They helped so much that for months of continual reading, I felt invincible. As you might guess, the invincibility faded, and I soon resumed my usual cycle: emotional highs and lows. As I look back now, I see how those early experiences introduced me to an important stage: learning how to feel better about what felt like a wound.

My Wounds

We each have our clay – our wounds, fears, passions and interests. The clay is those malleable parts of us that we use to begin our inner work. Wounds, for example, are wonderful blessings because when we accept them, we can allow the gifts they provide to us. Having wounds isn't the only way to discover a need for acceptance. Wounds are an obvious point of initiation into acceptance. Some of my wounds were the fear of making mistakes (fear of guilt), fear of being verbally attacked, fear of not reaching my potential (fear of failure), and fear of remaining emotionally suppressed, and yet, I still had a relatively normal and healthy childhood by most standards.

Somewhere along the line, I must have decided that to be strong, to make it in the world, I had to create one hell of a defense so that my wounds wouldn't be threatened. This determination was a factor in leading me to self-help books to understand myself and other people. It would also help me develop a good defense for any insecurity or wound I may have felt.

While these avenues provided some self-development and self-acceptance, I never shook off all of the wounds. Wounds were sometimes elusive and had a weird way of transforming into other wounds. This played a part in leading me to create (sometimes grand) accomplishments and competition with others as self-validating and compensating behaviors for whatever wound (insecurity) they had covered up.

I enjoyed genuine desires and passions in life, including the creative expression of making art, playing guitar and journaling. I played sports with friends and had healthy and strong social ties. I followed with each genuine desire, trusting that my guidance would lead me to a good place. Using the tools I'd developed (intuition and analysis), I did my best to thrive.

In my mid-twenties, I began to see more clearly the subconscious wounds that my behaviors inevitably covered up, but I had no idea how to fix them. The pursuit of uncovering and healing these wounds became important to me and, in part, led to the creation of this book.

Understanding Acceptance

Years into my work in the field of self-development, I realized that many of my efforts seemed to be guided by motivating forces other than my conscious choices. The books I read in my teens touched on the topic of the subconscious mind, but I quickly realized that I needed to research it more deeply. Still, I felt certain there was more to spiritual discovery than subconscious motivations. So, armed with what I understood (mentally and intuitively), I set out to find my answers once more.

At this point, my approach to growth was "understand to accept." This motto served me well—until I noticed that much of my self-acceptance stemmed from a mental level, not an emotional level. The rabbit hole went deeper yet, for even as I gained knowledge of spiritual psychology, I made little progress in becoming a better spiritual student. There was far too little correlation between my understanding and my actual self-acceptance.

Beyond the Mind

I began to discover a startling concept: my mind alone could not lead me to spiritual freedom. My efforts to try harder to figure things out only made the answers more difficult to find. With effort, I did learn, but I was forcing my way—not gliding gracefully. After many years of struggle, I realized that pushing harder only made things worse. As a result, I finally accepted the advice that I had heard all along from spiritual books, my friends, and my inner guidance, which had urged: Relax. Relaxing was how I would go beyond the mind.

I felt weary about embracing more seriously my emotional wounds and going beyond the mind, so I let my foot off the gas pedal for a while. Growth was getting harder. It wasn't anymore about just feeling good or choosing the high road. It meant being willing to give up parts of myself that were based in illusion. There were things inside of me that seemed more sensitive and harder to accept and love. Still, my desire and guidance continued to urge me in that direction of self-discovery.

My Changing God

It was my choice to continually dig deeper to find answers about myself and to do it in my way. I felt that God always supported what I chose, though there was nothing special about my path. It was the one that felt the most natural to me. I knew no other way. My path was mine because it included my wounds and my passions. There is only the path that we inevitably walk—because it includes everything we are, and the more it embraces 'everything we are,' the more fulfilling the path.

My path yielded experiences I considered "mistakes." They were not mistakes; they helped me learn. While it was always possible to make measurable mistakes as defined by rules, I felt that spiritually speaking, a mistake was merely a judgment. What was judgment? I believed in my heart that God did not judge me, though the belief that He (She or It) judged sure was popular. Over time, I saw that I judged myself plenty and did not need anyone's help with that task. Taking it a step further, I began to feel that my self-judgments and guilt determined how I believed God treated me.

With more reading and study, it seemed evident to me that a judging God was based upon the person whose ideas characterized Him that way. In other words, if I felt guilty, then I believed that God thought I was guilty. If I felt loving, then I felt that God loved me. The fascinating thing I discovered was that both viewpoints of guilt and love seemed to be true at different times. This led me to believe that any belief I had about God or anyone else was closely tied to whatever I could accept about myself.

Until then, spiritual growth had meant focusing on accepting only the things that were "good" about me, which meant I was accepting only part of me—not accepting the part that felt guilty.

Playing Games

Because I'm human, many times, I have fallen off my path. I've wrestled around in the dark with a flashlight, looking for a shred [of truth] that my mind could hold onto when all I needed to do was relax and let go. In many situations, I have over-thought things, garnered false sources of strength, boasted my ego identity, and blinded myself to the larger view. Also, I've many times been narrow-minded and non-accepting. I have been and continue to be, at times, a victim to the ego's influence. The main difference now is that I do not as often judge myself and hold myself guilty for allowing this to happen. Each time I let go of the guilt, I garner a little more acceptance.

After all of my work trying to overcome my guilt-enforcing ego, an astonishing realization surfaced: fighting against the ego made me lose the internal struggles. It strengthened the fight within me and resolved nothing. So many things I had rallied for or against now looked like mere justifications for the fight I had been already fighting within. This was a game I did not need to play.

Accepting Wounds

When we come into this life, we have deliberately chosen the potentiality of the wounds we carry as well as the gifts those wounds can develop within us. This book is one small result of using some of those wounds to discover more self-acceptance. For years I condemned the parts of me that I didn't like so I could feel that I was embracing a higher ideal for myself. This approach to spiritual acceptance is flawed because it is subject to the divisive ego within. It is an approach that disallows total acceptance. So long as I accept parts of me while refusing to accept others, I am conflicted, and the acceptance is not true acceptance.

For years, studying the ego became a high priority for me, among other important themes like "surrendering." So I delved deeply into studying *A Course in Miracles*. That's when the hard-core inner work started. It involved no other people or groups, just me. The hole went deeper in revealing just how many games I played, which I didn't even know I played with myself and others.

Using myself as a guinea pig, I debunked some of my ego's tricks, increasing my awareness and helping others benefit along the way. Ironically, I discovered that I had also strengthened my own ego because the one game that I wouldn't give up was where I allowed ego to stand between me and my self-acceptance occasionally. That is, when I allowed ego to be the director of my spiritual agenda. Whenever I felt that my spirit was under the influence of heavy agenda, I knew that I was no longer in spirit and led by God but led by ego.

Surrender

Surrender became ever more important to implement. There seemed to be no true escape from ego because every attempt somehow involved ego at the subtle levels. My eventual realization of this made me feel like I had been putting out fires with gasoline instead of water. In short, I couldn't accomplish much on my own. Surrendering to God was looming as the only real way for any chance at lasting freedom, and even then, maintenance was always required to prevent ego's constant attempts to infiltrate.

Surrendering was easy and fun with simple things, but I was afraid to give up control with important things. "Importance" seemed to disguise the fact that I felt fear and, yet, whatever I had surrendered regularly flowed easily in my life. Thus, whenever I have successfully stopped playing the bargaining game with what I've surrendered to God, I have always been able to deeply enjoy myself, other people, and know the acceptance of myself and the peace of God.

God is incredibly simple, and yet how simple God is depends upon how challenging and complex I've made my approach to Him. For example, I've wanted to understand many things about God, but understanding hasn't been necessary for me to know God. Surrender is the work-around or the bypass so that I don't have to do all of the extra work on my own. Whenever I forget and feel fearful, surrender has been my way back to trusting and accepting me in God.

When I've surrendered, it has meant that I have trusted in God. It has meant that I have accepted. Instead of "understanding to accept," I have "accepted to understand." In surrender, I have allowed many good things and good people into my life because my mind accepted without the need for understanding. That's why God is so good. It is because when we learn how to let Him lead us, we have the opportunity to quicken our path back home to Him.

The Aim of this Book

In this book, I'd like to share some of the insights and foibles along my path in learning acceptance and discovering my connection to God—my Source within—as each of us must do. To this day, I still discover insights, and I still have shortcomings, but I quicken the process with each step as I give that step to God. I've discovered that I don't have to do anything except remove my resistance, relax and allow.

This book teaches that. The writing in this book will vary in terminology since it was originally written over six years. However, I have updated the essays a great deal to round out the rough edges and fortify the messages with my current awareness while preserving their integrity.

I invite you to question each part of this book for yourself. If something does not feel right to you to accept, then don't accept it! If it does feel right, then accept it! There's no need to put any focus upon something that does not feel appropriate for you. What is appropriate will feel good to you. What is not, won't. Let your feelings of truth ringing inside of you be your guide. Beyond that, you'll have to decide for yourself whether what you are reading is inappropriate for your growth or if it challenges you to open up and stretch your mind to accept.

Since there is no wrong way to live a spiritual life, there are infinite paths we can create and walk, and all are equally honored. However we choose to live, just being here to experience is enough. What we make of life beyond just being here to experience, expand and express is purely optional.

Please accept this book as a brief testimony of some of the insights I have garnered along my path until this point in time. I offer it in loving acceptance of you and your path. Whatever your religious practices or spiritual beliefs, it is my prayerful intention that this book assists you in understanding and accepting your connection to the God Source within you that loves us and connects us all.

Self-Acceptance

Autopilot, Self-Worth and Being Myself

Family Weekend

I remember visiting my mom while my brother's family was staying at her house. We played some games together and had a good time. My wife and I ended up sleeping over since the drive there was a long one, and we stayed up late socializing. After a comfortable sleep on a futon mattress, we woke up the following day to continue our visit. Our family sleeping overnight in the same house created a unique circumstance the following day.

After what would be considered some relatively normal morning interaction, I noticed a peace beginning to envelop me that made me want to extend our visit. I could say that everyone's defenses were down, but that wouldn't be accurate since we're an open and supportive family. Yet, the interactions with my family were somehow fresher, clearer. What was it?

No Autopilot

What I think happened was that we interacted without running on autopilot. In our context, "autopilot" meant interacting with each other using preprogrammed mental conditioning instead of genuine interaction. Switching off autopilot meant not being afraid of showing who we truly were to each other. The freshness of my family's unscripted morning interactions yielded more openness and higher quality than if we had spent an entire day apart before gathering. We didn't have any time to get into our normal mental conditioning and filters before we interacted.

I began to have insights into what was shifting as I observed the changing quality of our time spent together. My family and I are already close, but we bonded even more closely on that second day because we spent some time in different surroundings from which we were accustomed. I've found that choosing a neutral location as the gathering place and changing the activities helps us express ourselves more naturally without falling into outdated roles and perceptions of each other, which keeps interactions stagnant.

Shortchanging Ourselves

So many times, my expressions have been stuck on autopilot and, therefore, have been uncreative. I find it fascinating that while we all have brilliance to express, we reveal little about ourselves. Why is that?

One reason is that we want to prove to ourselves that we are strong or that we know something. We seem to be a little more comfortable after we affirm to ourselves that we know something. Another possibility is that we may feel that to produce something valuable, we must produce something profound or intellectual.

Could it be that we have an ongoing conditioned pretense with ourselves? We all have an identity that we uphold,

4

something about ourselves that we project onto the world. It could even be, "Hey, look at how spiritual I am!" Is that a true representation of the level of self-acceptance that we have for ourselves? That we must *produce* or *achieve* to be of value? That we must build up our ego to develop self-esteem and self-worth?

Self-Worth

An interesting definition of self-worth came to me this weekend while talking to a friend. "Self-worth means how much it is *worth* to you to be yourself." In that definition, self-worth had nothing to do with how well or how much or how deeply I could do something. It meant, "How much are you willing to put yourself through before you decide just to *be yourself?*" "Is it worth *not* being you?" When we have little self-worth, we don't believe that being ourselves is good enough or worthwhile. That doesn't only mean to *feel unworthy*. It could also mean that we might spend a lot of our time trying to be something other than who we are, meaning non-acceptance of ourselves. Sometimes, we do such a great job of being someone else instead of just being ourselves that we wonder why things don't work out for us. We lose touch with our authenticity and creativity. That's a self-worth issue, too, only buried and harder to recognize.

Practicing Mastership through Self-Acceptance

When we practice our mastership, we aren't afraid to be ourselves. When we practice mastership, we don't defend; we aren't afraid to respond to others authentically, admit when we're afraid or that we have fears. We're just being ourselves without hiding underneath pretentious identities.

Over the years, I've watched myself try on various beliefs but now recognize them as substitutions for just being me. It is human nature to identify ourselves with things or ideas to know the difference between who we are and everything else. Unfortunately, when something important is at the forefront of our minds (career, appearances, etc.), we tend to freeze into paralysis. Whatever we're attached to owns us.

I certainly do have some fears, such as a fear of making mistakes (the fear of guilt) and a fear of not being seen for who I am. I've surrendered and healed some of those fears over time (although I am a continual work in progress). Having the courage to feel and release those programs yields high rewards. Time and again, I have believed that I had reached an impasse in a relationship, only to find that truthfully I was reaching an impasse within myself. It was then that I went head to head with the discomfort of some limitation that was stopping me from stepping forward. Whether I rationalized it or condemned it, it was still something I had not yet accepted. With a lot of trial and error, I discovered that I could release a limitation enough to accept myself more and thus accept a relationship at a higher level of maturity.

The End of Our Rope

When we think we're at the end of our rope, we're at *the beginning of real growth*. We are *not* at the end of a relationship when we have a big fight; we are at the *beginning* of an opportunity to make it a more conscious relationship. That which hurts us the most we see as an "end" because we cannot see past the fears we haven't yet released. All paths continue on the other side of our limitations, but we don't always choose to walk that far. There is an entire universe of possibilities for expanded choices and healthy living beyond what fear makes us believe we can't access. If we choose to go beyond fear, we'll discover an inner strength that we've never known before.

False Labels

We are all spiritual beings, yet we don't always believe it. I remember how excited I was to call myself "spiritual" because I enjoyed reading spiritually-themed books. I attached to the label before I was even aware of what real internal transformation involved. I played with lofty spiritual themes and abilities because they were fun, I had the aptitude, and I didn't have to grow that much. It was a hobby.

It is astonishing to recognize how easy it is to confuse accepting something with resisting something. For example, actions masquerading as spiritual growth can be weaponized to bury or project pain, and it can happen at any level of development. We wonder why our ministries don't grow larger until we discover how we've been fooling ourselves into developing only the parts of us that our egos wanted to develop while rejecting the parts that needed development.

It's easy to be a fan of anything spiritually related, especially when it's light and fun, but real growth includes embracing and accepting all of those dusty, dark corners of the heart. If we say we're growing, but our life isn't improving, can we take another honest look at what "growth" means?

Release your illusions. Cutting down a tree still leaves the roots, even though we cannot see them. Tracing our emotional and psychological roots will reveal just how much is illusion about "who we think we are." This is a lifelong process of gaining awareness and delicately recognizing and accepting the roots. The results of such inner work are more than worthwhile since what we are giving up is false and what we are gaining is the peace of God.

Comfortable in Our Skin

Let's nurture those instances when we are not running on autopilot when we're not afraid to speak as ourselves. Those we admire are the most comfortable being themselves and accept us for who we are regardless of what we do. It is said that a teacher is someone who is expressive of love. Look for that quality first if you feel the need or desire to learn from a teacher other than yourself.

When we are not comfortable being ourselves, and when we can't write the checks of our acceptance, we analyze, we pick apart, we feel threatened, we try to prove ourselves, we hang on the words of others. We are in an insane state most of the time. Some of us merely are better at controlling it than others.

Accept being a Little Crazy

Accept it. Accept the fact that sometimes (or perhaps a lot of the time) we feel weird about ourselves, we focus on what we don't want, we don't know what the hell is happening to us, we build a bigger ego, and we feel a general discomfort. Henry David Thoreau once said that most people live lives of quiet desperation. It's even truer for how we feel about ourselves. How we truly feel about ourselves is usually buried a few layers beneath our auto-responsive conditioning ("autopilot"). We need to get into touch with that to be true to ourselves.

Ever think about what it would be like to be successful for *being you*?

Being Ourselves

We always benefit more when we speak from the heart rather than perform aerial acrobatics that others may require. The shallower we are, the more easily we are dazzled by appearances. We succumb to advertising when it promises us a shred of personal power and a more defined sense of self. But it is far less costly just to be ourselves. It is the most natural thing we can do. If we play to the world, we play to the illusion. But if we play to our song, we help the world by default. I strive to be me, but sometimes it's difficult. Some things will always be new and unknown to me because I don't know what I don't know. I just have to take it in stride, embrace the unknown and learn. The more I return to just being me as I embrace the new, the more my life flows because I'm not peddling anything that I am not.

True vs. False Success

True success happens when we follow the desire and passion of who we want to be despite appearances. False success offers quicker external gain but at the expense of losing touch with ourselves. In false success, we are stuck with the same disease that caused us to take that path, to begin with. We aren't healed. We haven't "made it" anywhere, although appearances may imply otherwise. Quick success is unstable because it is based on commodity rather than true value, and I find that many people confuse the two. In false success, a person is puzzled when a successful plateau is followed by a downfall, implying that what they did warranted attention but had no lasting value. Could true success be so detrimental?

Planting Seeds

We can enjoy true success when we relinquish the need to capture the stage's attention and instead star in our own lives. There is nothing more satisfying than harvesting the fruit from the seeds that we plant. In so doing, we get to enjoy all of the fruits that we had once carefully planted within ourselves and nourished along the way. When we honor our paths by planting seeds of value, we develop personal power, do what we love, are genuine, avoid autopilot, and are true to ourselves. We make continual good decisions because each step of the way is a seed we plant and a fruit we harvest with God.

Being a Conscious Example

Making Our Feelings Known

Our world operates so fast that we tend to lose touch with our feelings and the practice of expressing them. Expressing our real feelings truthfully *is* spiritual, and it creates transformation through the body, a necessary part of spiritual development. This expression (versus suppression) is a way of practicing honesty within ourselves. It's a simple practice, it makes us feel good, and life runs smoother when we do it regularly.

So why do we have the pretenses? We're afraid that someone will "find us out." We're afraid that we won't be accepted if we give our real opinions or afraid that we won't be thought of as highly if we let others know how upset something made us. In response to this, I lovingly suggest that expressing ourselves is incredibly spiritual because it creates personal, social and cosmic transformation. Sharing how we feel is very, very important.

It's Okay to Have Needs

One of the reasons (besides fear) that we are such pretentious beings is the notion that once we have embarked upon a path or embraced a role (especially a spiritual one), we make it virtually unacceptable for ourselves to have needs. We

11

think we must master anything we undertake right away as if being incredibly spiritual or good at what we do means having no needs. It doesn't.

As physical beings, we *do* have needs: needs for intimacy, needs for interaction, needs for being understood, needs for love and needs for sustenance. By acknowledging and embracing our needs, we are practicing self-acceptance. We are not weak for paying attention to our needs. We are wiser and more mature for identifying and nurturing them. Nurturing our needs fosters the proper development of life. Adults need just as much food, love and support as small children do. Taking care of oneself is important, just as developing emotional independence important, but a healthy personal definition of spiritualism is the embracing of what one needs. Accepting our own needs is a demonstration of independence and spiritual strength. Spiritual independence is not eliminating needs; it is in knowing what you need, accepting that you need it and allowing yourself to have it.

How We Use Beliefs

We can easily fall into the trap of unconsciousness as we wear our belief systems such as spiritualism and religion. These beliefs may be spiritual indeed, but they are subject to variation, depending on *how* we use the belief. We can perform any action, but behind the action may be several different motivations: compassion, condemnation, fear, joy, disappointment. These motivations are invisible on the surface but range from love to violence underneath. If we use our beliefs to create acceptance or unification and genuinely feel better, then our beliefs serve our needs. If we use our beliefs as defense and separation, our beliefs are not serving our needs.

Find the Root Energy

I used to think that addressing someone's problem required an explanation to help them become aware. Sometimes an explanation was helpful; other times, it wasn't. If we were close to addressing the underlying root energy, then our discussion was more helpful. I've come to discover that what some call the 'sponsoring thought,' or the 'root energy' of what is being expressed is the real catalyst for transmutation. When we operate intuitively, we can feel this resonance in other people, places and things. We can feel what root energies are being harbored when we place our consciousness there.

Awareness of Ego and Unconsciousness

Unconsciousness is being unaware. It is represented by ego. At its core, ego is fear. It is built in as a protection mechanism, but it becomes unconscious when we mistake it for our real identity. When we become unconscious and lose the connection to our presence, we lose touch with our feelings. We become led by what happened or what will happen. We feel as if life happens to us instead of us choosing what we want in life.

No matter how well disguised as support, ego will not necessarily bring about a release or solution. Somehow, someway, it will subtly perpetuate the problem. Ego will give us the illusion of a solution but coerce us to believe that something else also needs our attention, merely digging us deeper into believing that we have a problem. The more present we become, the more we can observe this dynamic occurring.

Being Yourself vs. Being Pretentious

The ego would have us believe that putting on a newer belief would make us more spiritual. Not true. While trying on new beliefs can lead us into the general direction of exploration and discovery, beliefs themselves are not responsible for transformation. Interchanging beliefs can become platitudes and serve as illusions of change. A platitude is everything ego would have us say in substituting a genuine response from our real self in any situation. Spiritually based platitudes are typically mental affirmations, reminders of what we believe without necessarily experiencing what lies beyond the belief. Although helpful, there comes a time when affirmations are no longer needed, and the light of our real responses, true feelings of love and gifts are called forth to be given to those who need to receive what we have to share.

In each situation, we can respond to life in a fashion that begets presence. A simple test of consciousness growth is to observe if your presence or actions within a conflict dissolves it or enflames it. Observance alone can work. We know that digging deeper into a negative situation will cause more strain. We know that detaching will create more perspective. Light will beget light. Consciousness will bring about consciousness.

Receiving Help from Others

When we are not self-aware, we are served best when another being can hold that space of presence for us. By doing so, they aren't required to do anything in particular for us except to hold the presence we want to reach. Their conscious presence provides the space for us to expand. Our negative energies within us know how to resolve themselves. However, when we have a supporter who can hold the space of presence when we have not yet learned how to do so in a particular area, we become self-aware more quickly. Sometimes, this saves us lots of time and trouble.

Holding a Space for Others

Through total acceptance of each person's level of development, we are in the best position to serve them in their consciousness growth. There is nothing wrong with what a person is learning, or if they are learning differently than we are. Each individual learns best when allowed to learn on his path, in his way.

There is a divine blueprint in each of us which provides us with what we are to learn. When we are in spiritual service, we will support what a person is learning by gently guiding them to *their* chosen path, not pushing them away from what they feel drawn to learn.

Staying Centered in Self

The goal for those committed to spiritual growth is to "know thy self," feel peace, be of service, stay centered in self, and remain connected to Source. This essay serves as an example of everyday situations that we can use to create consciousness growth, be a conscious example, and allow life to move through us with grace. Life is set up to serve us in whatever way we tune into it and ourselves to find our own unique ways of growth and centering.

Allowing God

17

Conscious Spiritual Teaching and Source-Aligned Service

Serving in Alignment with Source

When we feel a natural positive urge to be of service, we could call that 'serving in alignment with Source.' The feel-good vibe that we receive is the Source's blessing that it is an appropriate time to serve. This could be based on the person, time, place or any number of unknown reasons. Trusting these feelings of guidance to serve takes care of all of the details we do not need to know. When we are serving in alignment, it feels effortless to give and receive. It brings things into focus. We feel high-powered, as if the essence of our Source guidance is pouring through us like a faucet.

We must check in with our true feelings and ask our God Source within if it is appropriate for us to be of service. Aligning ourselves with Source in this way makes all of our service ordained. As we take a moment of stillness to listen within and act when we feel called to act, we are following our guidance from Source. Remember that guidance can come in all forms and may sometimes seem off the path that you feel you should follow. But if we follow the guidance with trust, the results will fortify everyone involved perfectly and better than we could have imagined.

It doesn't matter if anything we give is received by anyone

else in the way that we think. In aligned service, we are giving because it feels good to give. The act of giving is not done to receive something in return. We serve because we feel called to act.

The greatest thing about service in alignment is that we serve when asked to serve as indicated by listening to our feelings. At times it may seem that we are losing something; however, reality is to the contrary. *A Course in Miracles* teaches us that giving is the same as receiving, meaning: we are creating Source alignment no matter who's receiving externally. In heeding the call to serve, we maintain our connection to God because our service creates alignment for all involved. We will allow more good things by choosing to focus on what feels good to do, and service is just one example.

Serving in Misalignment with Source

In our misaligned service, we are forcing ourselves to serve in some way. Maybe we feel that we *should* be serving, or maybe someone expects us to serve. In misaligned service, we operate from mind, identity, conditioning and self-assigned roles. We put our thinking ahead of God's loving guidance. It is important to remember that true service is not done based on obligation. Service truly means offering what we are called to offer based on our feelings of positive guidance. It is not offering what we "think" is needed by our ego-mind's assessment alone. It takes practice because the feelings of compulsion provided by ego can make us think that it is in the person or situation's best interest to act from compulsion instead of guidance. For example, acting out of fear for someone does not mean that we are helping them.

Agenda vs. Service

As teachers, we can create confusion for a student if we impose our agenda over our service. A student looking for answers may not know how a spiritual answer looks or feels, so they are somewhat at the mercy of our teaching. Although some things are important to learn, we must understand when it is important to yield our agenda and allow students to determine the pace for learning while supporting their choices.

Ego's Imposition

When our ego becomes attached to how we serve, we allow our teaching to become an avenue for ego to strengthen itself. This can lead us into trouble. As teachers, we must be careful not to impose our guidance over someone else's guidance. Doing so can strengthen our ego at the expense of creating dependency in the student. As teachers, the goal is not to create reliance upon us but to create self-trust in the student.

The Compulsive "Should"

Our egos tell us that just because we *can* serve means that we *should* serve. When we follow the compulsive should, we cut ourselves off from our Source guidance. Our gifts are then in service to ego and not to God. Left unattended, the ego compulsion can turn into arrogance and smother our inner guidance. In other words, by not stopping to ask our inner guidance what is needed, we risk falling victim to ego's compulsive influence to strengthen itself through any means, including how we serve others. Furthermore, by enabling ego compulsion, we confuse ourselves as to Source guidance and ego influence. In so doing, we fall victim to ego's dominance over our consciousness.

Boast and Cover

Ego loves to find a way to "boast and cover." We boast about what our ego wants to flaunt while we conveniently cover up our insecurities. It'sa "win-win" scenario for ego but a spiritual growth inhibitor that can be difficult to give up. In boasting, we give the impression that we are confident, but underneath, we may feel inadequate. It can be difficult to resist the urge to voice our opinion when we feel strongly. Yet, ego tells us that this "strong" feeling is confidence when it may only be self-righteousness and plain insecurity—ego in sheep's clothing.

We "build around the wound" instead of healing it in hopes that no one will be inclined to witness the wound's presence. The stronger the wound, the more insistent we might be in giving no impression whatsoever that we have anything resembling the wound that we most want to hide. Curiously, however, our defense mechanisms such as the "boast and cover" example are intimately tied to the nature of our wounds. Our egos want us to avoid our pain to the point where we may even fool ourselves so completely that we thinkwe don't even have the wounds.

I have fallen victim to my ego on countless occasions. Although I have taught others with the utmost sincerity and responsibility at any stage, my ego was still subconsciously looking for validation and security underneath my service to some extent. My ego had me believing that I was teaching for

God, but I wasn't necessarily teaching from God at all times. My underlying insecurities were influencing how I was teaching and the fact that I was teaching. Until these small yet potent subconscious motivations became conscious, I could not yet know that my perceptions required correction and healing. There is no judgment here, only a pointing out that awareness is the component that makes correction identifiable.

Trust Yourself, Not Me

It is highly common for seekers of spiritual answers to trust the guidance of a teacher over their guidance. We trust teachers so that they can help us trust ourselves. It may be extremely helpful to receive the assistance of someone's natural gifts or talents for healing, particularly when the gift creates alignment in the student. However, the error in perception occurs if the student places more value upon the teacher's guidance than the student's guidance. A teacher may be a trustworthy authority, but their everlasting duty is not to create adoration but to reflect responsibly the everlasting power of God abiding in each student.

God's Invitation

We can choose to wait for God's invitation and His feel-good blessing for us to serve instead of ego's want for validation. We can allow our natural ability to feel good inside to guide us into service instead of serving to receive approval. The mark of our qualification for service at any moment is by our receiving of God within us. Without that, we can only teach white magic. In other words, when we choose to first feel alignment before serving, we are then able to offer God to others.

Worthy Teaching

In teaching from worthiness, we feel God being expressed through our love and acceptance of ourselves and others. In teaching from unworthiness, we enable the substituted ego to attempt to prove our value. The problem is that we will never prove ego's value because, ultimately, ego does not exist. Attempting to do so would be a lifelong battle in a search for self-worth.

We mistake the ego's compulsive desire to prove our value as our sincere desire to serve. Proving our worthiness (or value) is unnecessary because we naturally feel worthy in our alignment with God. We prove our value as a substitute for self-acceptance, and yet there are faster ways to gain self-acceptance—by going straight to God in prayer, for example. In waiting for God's invitation to serve, we avoid the compulsions which enable ego to infiltrate our teaching.

Humility

A good antidote to ego's influence is learning humility. True service is a result of humility. It means to be on the earth but not of the earth. It means to live from the inside out instead of the outside in. It means to use the wellspring of God within as guidance and not use the inundation of worldly thinking as guidance. It means to give and not take, to share and not hoard.

When we recognize an opportunity to serve, it is because we

feel an outpouring of love in our hearts. In taking, our egos recognize an opportunity to feel stronger or better than, equaling more "confidence" by our ego's standards. In giving, the God in us recognizes an opportunity to be more loving. Humility is the foundation that guides us to the greatest spiritual service. It is the blessing from God which lets us know that we have something to offer and that offering is peace.

The End Justifies the Means

Before we have surrendered our minds to God, the compulsion that ego offers us is to share what we think we know. While we may indeed know something and while sharing what we know may be helpful, we still need to listen within carefully. We need to recognize and feel whether our intention to serve is to offer what is needed or bolstering what is known. Higher quality in service will entail recognizing and providing with more awareness what is needed. Without listening carefully within, we may fall victim to the ego's justification of itself. When our ego recognizes a circumstance in which it feels it can justify its intervention, it can trick us into believing that proving itself equals spiritual service.

Let's say I am a teacher whose ego has a compulsive need to prove that I have value and can help anyone. No doubt, I have developed some intuitive expertise in guiding people in resolving their issues. You and I attract, and we decide to work together. I help you gain some perspective. You feel that you received something of value from me because I was able to provide some insight to you, then we part company.

On one level, there was a natural success. The two of us attracted because we were both looking for the same thing—validation. On another level, there was a different dynamic occurring. My ego used the situation to strengthen itself and attempt to prove that it has value and that it is powerful. But the trade-off is that even compulsive ego needs which are soothed will return, and the ego will need to prove its value once again. The cycle of my non-acceptance continues.

From the student's perspective, he received the validation he wanted. However, he wasn't aware of my ego's agenda to strengthen itself. I helped him on one level. On another level, my ego has claimed its victory over me. This example introduces the need for conscious teaching.

Conscious Teaching Observations

In the past, I have been the soliciting compulsive teacher who honestly believed that his every word was out of service and who honestly believed that the world would freeze over if I weren't "serving my purpose." How untrue. My early intentions for service were well-meaning but undoubtedly riddled with my ego's control mechanisms and emotional suppression over my development, a trait relatively common for novice teachers. It seemed that my overzealousness usually had a suppressed counterpart. That is, until enough repetitive run-ins with my ego eventually revealed to me that I wasn't developing emotionally. I only thought I was.

It wasn't until I had seen the pattern recurring within my ego's need to "serve my purpose" that I had been masking my emotional development. This realization led me to conscious prayer for more humility. In recognition of what was not working for me, I chose to surrender control to God to teach me a better way when I had decided that I "had enough." Through desire, prayer, self-observation and more conscious practice of what I preached, I recognized my misalignments in service with more definition and was, therefore, able to address them. In choosing to face that not all of my actions had come from guidance, but some had come from the compulsion to act, my awareness yielded to me the capacity to observe the dynamic in other teachers. This is because what we truly face in ourselves, we no longer subconsciously work to cover up.

Wearing the Mask

I have witnessed talented teachers continue to ask for validation even after their service had been politely refused. Some knew they were wearing a mask at some level of awareness, and some didn't seem to know. It eventually became abundantly clear how easy it is for us teachers to mistake the seeking out of ego validation as a substitute for the acceptance of Source alignment as our fuel for service. With recognition comes consciousness awareness and, of course, more effective teaching.

The Need for Service

Accepting that we have needs is accepting that we need love, and fulfilling our needs is accepting love. We all need to serve, and we all need to be served. We need love. Teachers need love. We need validation and approval sometimes, and that's okay because it's what we need. We need to be told we did a good job. We need to receive any morsel of love that helps us to accept ourselves. We need to recognize the difference between a person who is ready and asking for self-acceptance and a person who is not. We need to step in and offer peace at the moment anyone is ready to receive it.

Responsibility of Teachers

As teachers, we are not destined to put out fires but teach others how not to create them. Our humility teaches us that we are just as much a student to any student we teach at any moment and that our teaching others never negates their teaching us. When we speak, we need to remember to be in alignment before offering assistance. At the core of the students' questions is the desire to learn how to trust the God in them. The only thing worth teaching is love and peace, and no matter how we convey it, we need to remember that, in our service, we are first and foremost in total service to God.

Time For Yourself

Why We Need It

Do you take regular time out for yourself? A mentor once told me that it's important for us to meditate every day, in some form. Whether it's for fifteen minutes, thirty minutes, or an hour, meditation helps us to center and balance ourselves, allowing us the time to address our day with clear energy. Without doing so, we may continue remembering the stress we took with us the day before and continue escalating it. And let's face it, how we do everything is the most important reason for doing anything. How determines the quality of our lives.

Am I Doing It Right?

A preoccupation that many of us have is whether or not we are meditating correctly. Unfortunately, this belief of whether or not we are doing something the "right" way stops us from doing it. No method applies to everyone. There is only the method that helps each of us to relax. There is a unique recipe for each of us, and that recipe is whatever way we feel works the best for us personally, and that's good enough. Isn't that refreshing?

Methods of Relaxation

For me, driving in my car with some peaceful music or sounds of nature in the CD player relaxes me. Sitting in a quiet room with candlelight and incense burning is another option. Even listening to music during an exercise workout may create stillness and relaxation. Anything that helps us calm down and relax is a meditative practice.

Benefits

Within days of meditating regularly, we will feel a difference in our experience. Food may taste better, sleep quality may increase, and interactions may become more positive. With more practice will come greater self-mastery. We may find that we had been able to sit quietly for only 10 minutes in the beginning. After a few weeks or months, however, we may be able to sit for much longer periods and in much deeper levels of stillness and peace. The deeper we go, the more there is to gain.

Mental Surrender

You may find at first that the mind resists meditation regularly. It wants to keep thinking and planning. It wants to stay in control, but you will find that the mind will eventually begin to surrender its resistance if you sit there anyway. The relaxing feeling is your proof that the mind has let go. This is a key point in arriving at deeper levels of relaxation and stillness. When the mind learns to surrender control and no longer resists meditation, you will relax and go deeper with increasing quickness and quality.

Detoxification

Many people stop once they find that meditation yields some kind of discomfort. But these are signs that nature is taking its course. As we allow space for the mind to be still, it begins its mental and emotional detoxification process. Unprocessed feelings, emotions, memories and situations arrive into our awareness, asking to be felt to be released as a part of our mental and emotional detoxification. Just because we don't feel our emotions regularly doesn't mean they're not present within us. Layers upon layers of unprocessed emotions which we've pushed down and haven't accepted may begin to arrive into our awareness to await purification.

In most cases, it is not important to focus on what arrives but to recognize it from an observer's perspective. Just allow the things that arrive to be there as they come up and continue to breathe through them. All you have to do is breathe and allow.

Breathing

Your breath is perhaps the most important thing in managing detoxification and in creating stillness. Your breath is the conduit that carries away all of the toxicity in your mind, body and energy. If your body is like a vehicle and the food you eat is like the fuel that powers your vehicle, breathing is like performing a regular oil change for your vehicle. Oil may not be the actual fuel that makes your vehicle move, but without oil, your vehicle would eventually break down from too much toxicity.

Good meditative breathing practices can train our mind and body to relax through our day. How we breathe is our reminder of how much stress we are feeling. Are we breathing shallow and nervously or deep and calmly? Recognizing the quality of our breathing during our waking consciousness can be like a measuring stick for when we need to relax and meditate.

A Goal Worth Achieving

Whether we are standing in an elevator, arriving at work a few minutes early, or playing with our children and pets, any practice that relaxes us can be meditative. As we remember to take time for ourselves, we are maintaining ourselves in an exceptionally healthy manner. However, if we do not, we may fall victim to the overworked mind's agenda, which insists that we "get everything done" before we can relax—a ploy by which no end will ever be in sight.

We deserve more than the promise of an ending from the chattering mind. We deserve more than to settle for our incessant thinking to determine by default how we will react. Instead, we deserve to experience joy, love and peace as we get things done. Creating stillness and relaxing the mind is always worthwhile and can drastically improve which actions we decide upon. Each time we choose to take a few minutes for ourselves, we are saying yes to our health, yes to our power to make good decisions, and yes to our ability to change the quality of our lives.

Experience the Ripple

Have you ever skipped down the street? It's quite enjoyable. Now imagine skipping as if you are on the moon. You are still skipping, but you begin to leap high and move slowly with each skip you take. Now, imagine that you are skipping along calm water. You see your reflection as you skip. It doesn't matter how deep the water is because you're only skipping on the surface. You begin to feel that you are surfing in a flow of energy that allows you total freedom. You now have freedom from gravity and freedom from sinking. Skip joyfully across the water with me for a while.

Feel how weightless you are as you skip along. Your toes barely touch the water, creating a small ripple each time you step. You dance joyously because you are just skipping along in the light of your soul. Let's say that you wanted to touch the water a bit more. Let's say that you want to experience how the water feels on your feet while you skip along the surface. So, you allow your feet to be submerged in the water as you skip. The ripples increase in size. Wow, that feels refreshing! You breathe deeply and enjoy it even more. There's nowhere in particular you'd like to go. You're just skipping because it feels good to you.

What if we completely submerged ourselves into the water? Would it be a bit scary? Would it be a fun experience? You believe that it would be a fun experience, so you stop and go underwater for a short while. The experience is exhilarating, and you create a huge ripple. "Wow, what a wonderful experience! I feel so refreshed," you say. So maybe you decide to jump in and out of the water over and over as you skip, like a dolphin, creating many ripples in the water. The deeper you go under, the farther your ripples reach out. You begin to take the best feeling you felt from skipping above the water, from letting your feet touch the water, and from submerging into the water, and you roll it all together for an even more exciting experience.

How does it feel to dangle your feet in the water every day? Do you sometimes submerge yourself? If you do, is it by accident or on purpose? Let's say everything that happens to us that appears to be accidental is something that we create. Would we skip differently? How big are our ripples? Would we enjoy it when we submerge? When you submerge, do you feel that you are sinking? Or do you enjoy the experience of how it feels? Why not do both? Why not appreciate how good it feels to be underwater, even if you didn't plan on getting wet?

We can skip across the water and never touch it. We can also skip alongthe water, touch the water, and experience how the water feels. Or, if we are bold, we can completely dive into the full experience of going underwater. Going underneath the surface might seem a little scary at first, but it is way more fun because you get wet! The ripples that you create will be far-reaching.

Seek First the Kingdom of God

What is our Divinity?

One of the intriguing misconceptions about our divinity is that it is something that we earn or achieve. However, being a Divine Human is not a pedestal concept reserved for enlightened beings and ancient masters. We are not separate from them, except in our thinking. What makes us divine is remembering to choose our divinity, just as the masters chose it for themselves.

We cannot escape our divinity because it is what makes us up at our core. It is what resides beneath the many layers of conditioning of how we have learned to behave. When we unlearn these layers, our divinity naturally shines through us. Yet, that inhibitor is our thinking.

The Mental Barrier

Our mind is a helpful companion when it is surrendered and relaxed. When the mind is relaxed, it is in alignment and allowing divinity to come forth. However, when we allow the mind to run the show, its noise keeps the divine from shining through us.

The mind is designed for survival and safety and, thus, is primarily programmed to reinforce itself. Even when reprogrammed, it tends to default back to its self-protection or, spiritually speaking, back to a state of non-trust.

When our mind isn't in fight or flight mode, it does a good job of helping us live our daily lives. Our mind facilitates our growth and follows our directions. It enables our "doing," which promotes our way of "being." It is the vehicle through which our divine nature is expressed. However, our mind is not the destination of our growth.

We can use the mind to accomplish pertinent tasks during our life, but we cannot expect it to live our life for us. When we are operating from the mind, we are in a state which does not encourage consciousness expansion. When it is utilized as a mode of being beyond our needs for immediate survival, the mind can suffocate our sacred presence and unknowingly rob us of our trust in our divine nature.

Going Beyond Mind

To grow individually and collectively, we desperately need to go beyond the mind to allow our divinity to be expressed. Thankfully, our mind has a built-in relationship with our body and spirit that constantly promotes and restores full and natural alignment in our beings despite our mind's resistance patterns. Therefore, we can go beyond the mind by helping it to relax and cooperate with our divinity.

The Mind as a Supplement

We use our brilliant mind involuntarily and as second nature in most cases. We do not always consciously choose to act from it. It usually chooses for us. It rarely occurs to us to "be" or operate in any other way unless we first filter things through our processing and evaluating system called the mind. It rarely occurs to us that there is another part of who we are, and yet we occasionally struggle to mentally look for these spiritual answers on Sunday mornings at church. If we do not find answers, it is because the place we were looking wasn't outside of our thinking.

We hope that our minds can grasp and understand where we look for answers and experience some relief. In reality, we are evolving our minds. But we tend to want to "go through" the mind before we allow ourselves to experience our divinity. Our minds are the turnpike through which we evaluate what we will allow inside our being and what we will allow to come out from us. Our minds alone are not designed to take us home to the promised land. Our minds do not substitute for our divinity. On the contrary, our minds supplement our divinity.

Am I only a Mind or Something More?

We are much more than the mind alone. We are the light of God. God is not separate from us. God is merely hidden beneath the mind. When we choose to relax the mind, we can go beyond it and see, feel and know this dwelling place of God within us. We can even use the mind to help us to fulfill the will of our divinity.

How does it feel to see a loved one after a long respite? How does it feel to give or receive a gift? These feelings are the light of God in you which have been allowed to shine through the mental barriers of normal mental conditioning. When we choose divinity repeatedly, it allows us to experience so much more of the light of God within us.

The Gift of Divinity

The greatest gift our divinity provides us is the real truth about who we are when we subordinate our minds and commit to divinity with full decision. We have all had those experiences which give us a taste of what is behind the illusion. As we continue exploring different ideas, we develop a sense of knowing what feels most real and truthful. These feelings are more real than if we had made a mental assessment or an evaluation with our mind. By allowing ourselves to feel, we are allowing ourselves to know divinity. By learning how to quiet our minds and listen within, we can allow that divinity within our being to shine through us. We can learn how to hear the guidance of divinity through practice. We can learn how to provide peace to ourselves. We can learn that we can access our truth within ourselves rather than seek out external pacifiers. As a result, we become clearer in discovering what is rooted in the mind and what is rooted in divinity.

Returning to Divinity

Divinity means returning to our hearts and our feelings. In spiritual growth, we don't need to focus on reaching outward, but we need to focus on returning inward. This is the place of creation, abundance, healing, peace, and more. Efforts to venture into the past or future are typically substitutions that the mind offers us instead of accepting our present moment. This sacrifices our joyous feelings, which come from accepting the present moment as it is. We begin to notice where divinity will and will not follow us in our thinking through observations like these.

Remember When We Were Kids?

Many of us would give anything to be able to experience more joy. We want to experience that sense of wonder and awe as we did when we were children. Children fully accept the present. This way of being is a pure expression of the divine before the mind has infiltrated with its layers of thinking, teaching us that more thinking and projecting away from the now will bring us happiness. A child knows only the natural approach of feeling and accepting life and must be taught to choose differently to change that approach. When we return to our true nature of divinity through conscious choice and awareness, our inner world ignites once again. Our sense of feeling begins to increase, and we return to our joy. Our sense of aliveness and passion re-emerge. We realize that growing old into feeling joyless is a function of the mind we choose and not a function of the spirit.

Willingness to Go Forth

Sometimes we wonder concerning matters of spirituality when we cannot derive a sense of truth about our divinity from within our mind alone. This is because divinity deals with feeling, whereas facts appeal to the mind. The mind's primary interest is to increase its comfort level, but not change. In this way, the mind can fool us into believing that we are growing or changing when we are unwilling to surrender anything to our divinity. In other words, "control" exists so that the ego-mind can persuade us that we are on a journey, but as long as the mind remains in control, we are not moving ahead spiritually. Instead, the mind strives for its idea of perfection, which means "mastering manipulation of externals." This is why financial success is the "end of the road" in the mind's effort to preserve itself.

Divinity is Simple

Divinity is simple, but realizing its simplicity usually takes the mind a long, long time to accept. It would rather exhaust all of its resources to either earn its worthiness to accept itself or avoid acceptance altogether. We can circumvent "achieving" divinity when our aim is acceptance of anything. It is then that we discover new meaning and new awareness about our lives. We see ourselves from an entirely different and fresh perspective. The clarity that we gain by allowing our divine nature to surface allows us to see a clearer, expanded version of who we are.

Silent Simplicity

Our mind happily releases the burden of being overworked once it has surrendered. Our mind begins to see a being who stands silently with it, patiently waiting for the mind to relax. With this awareness in our quiet simplicity, we look in the mirror, and we see someone who is peaceful and courageous, living in trust beyond the mind. We develop a new definition of who we are, and we get to know ourselves deeper. We have a clearer picture of what we are and how much self-love we have. By looking beyond the mind, we have found the real us—the Divine Human, which is always there and needs no approval or permission of any kind.

There is a finite list of applications and capacities for our overworked minds. But our divine nature is limitless. Divinity is our sovereign nature. It is within each of us, yet we are still learning how to allow ourselves to experience it. As we surrender our mind's control to our divinity, we begin to experience everything in life with more richness and vitality. As a result, our quality of life takes on a whole new dimension.

The Kingdom of God

We seek first the kingdom of God within ourselves. We learn how we operate in mind, body and spirit. We realign ourselves with the Divine. Beneath all of those layers of who we thought we were resides pure love at our core, waiting for us. Divinity is who we are now and what we will always be. We need to choose it.

God's Thoughts Are Real

Truthful Discovery

As we each continue to discover more truth on our path, we bounce around less among the unreal identities about who we believe ourselves to be. We discover more of ourselves as we discover more truth. We recognize ourselves when we remember what is truthful and not built upon illusion.

Like most, I have difficulty distinguishing what is real and what is not real, especially within me. This is because so many things I have learned about myself which I thought were true aren't necessarily true. Yet, I have found that in my practice of vigilance, the picture becomes much clearer.

I have found that we don't need to do the same things we once had done to get the same results we once had in how we feel about ourselves. God's truth is larger than our ego's agenda for how we try to make ourselves feel good. We do the same things because they bring us the same results of comfort and familiarity, but there's a more truthful layer beneath that which draws out our expressive spirit.

Where is the Truth?

When we are not feeling how we want to feel, we are quick to determine what we need to do to fix how we feel. While we're in this state of mind, we can learn to recognize it as being in a state of untruth because trying to fix things tends to pacify more than it creates acceptance.

When we are feeling bad, we have a hard time recognizing truth because the lack we feel begs us to reach *outward* to try to fix it. When we reach out in lack and feelings of untruth, we tend to whine that we are not where we are "supposed to be" in our growth. This approach offers us no freedom from our illusions.

Recognition of Choice

Essentially, when we recognize that we are in a state of illusion (or feeling untruth), we deal with fear more effectively. Our simple recognition of fear drives it away. This is far more effective than throwing layers of external fixes on top of fear. When we're trying to cope with fear, we comfort ourselves with food, for example. I've done my share of emotional eating.

But when we learn to recognize our thoughts of untruth, fear and negativity, we become instantly aware. With recognition, we awaken to our mastery because we now know that we can choose differently. Becoming aware that we have other choices is a form of consciousness growth.

No matter what fear, illusion or problem we are facing, there is a way to discover the truth within it. Once we recognize that we have a choice, we are no longer confused about our mastership. Our mastership means that our free will cannot be violated unless we allow the untruth that is fear to convince us otherwise. God gave us freedom, so we can thereby entertain any thoughts we wish, even ones that are untrue and keep us in pain and separated from ourselves, each other and Him.

Uncovering New Truth

Excitement happens when we experience something more truthful about ourselves than what we have come to know thus far. It can be liberating and inspiring to uncover a truth that we hadn't before recognized. This is one way that we release old ideas and illusions about ourselves. But truth is also a double-edged sword. It can be upsetting and scary when we discover a truth about ourselves that does not seem to be liberating and inspiring (at first) because we had been choosing not to face the truth.

Accepting Truth

Resistance and acceptance tend to be characteristics of our relationship with truth, meaning what we will accept or not accept about what we are facing. The interesting thing about acceptance and resistance is that they seem to indicate that we *do* know the truth, or we might not feel opposition either way. Therefore, we must ask ourselves if we are choosing to accept or resist what we know to be true.

It can be easy to miss the simple and silent spiritualism of using the feelings we have to learn where the truth resides in us. Our resistance and acceptance of anything indicates where our alignment is with what is occurring. Instead of abusing our feelings to circumvent truth, we can take a step forward *in* truth by choosing to accept what occurs as if we had chosen it. We may not feel guilty if we choose to avoid, but we will delay our spiritual journey and fool ourselves if we avoid acceptance.

God's Thoughts Are Real

Let us be vigilant to the awareness of what is true in our thoughts and what is not true by heeding those feelings of acceptance and resistance and using them as our teachers. By choosing this new level of self-honesty, we can strengthen our connection with truth. We will begin to understand which thoughts we think are the thoughts God would have us think, which thoughts have validity and carry us forward, and which do not. In choosing thoughts that lead us into truth, we can release the need to defend our illusions, believing we know more about ourselves than He does. Our spiritual expansion is a simple result of which thoughts we use to decide who we are. We are God's thoughts. His thoughts are real, and all power is of God.

Heart Is Where The Home Is

One afternoon, I gathered a few items together to take with me to visit at my dad's house. I remember stopping at my own house and taking inventory of what I would need to bring with me. At that time, I had been coming and going to and from my house so often that I had forgotten what it felt like to be at home. I began to notice how ungrounded I felt because of all of my frequent stops and running around.

I was putting something in my car when the thought came to me that said, "You are always exactly where you need to be." How true that was. I had forgotten that wherever I am, I am there by Divine Guidance. Before the insight came, I thought about when I would arrive at my dad's house and how much enjoyment I would feel when I got there. At that moment, however, I forgot that the enjoyment that I bring with me into each moment is what creates the quality of my experience.

I sat for a moment and enjoyed the peace that the insight washed over me. I forgot about worrying about the future and my haste and sank peacefully into the moment. I became silent and remembered that where I was located had no bearing on the amount of joy that I was allowing myself to experience at that moment. I stopped rushing to pack my things. There was nowhere else that I needed to be. There was no scarcity of time to get my packing completed. There was only my now moment experience and being where I was.

I navigated joyfully through my peace and was reminded of something else, which I felt was enlightening: home is where the heart is. It made me feel good to think about how much love exists around my home during the holidays. It is easy for us to imagine how comfortable we feel in our homes with our families, friends or loved ones. It is a well-known association that we feel good in such comforting places. Then, I felt the words change. "The heart is where home is." How interesting! Could it be that we always have the opportunity to be in our hearts? Our home environment is just an extension of our energy, a refuge, a place to center and balance ourselves. But it is through our hearts that we feel at home when we are home. When we think of our homes or loved ones, we begin to feel their energies as well. Do you, perhaps feel comfortable and at home watching football in your friend's basement? Or do you feel at home visiting your sibling's home and spending quality time there? I think there is much truth in that our hearts are where we feel at home. But we don't always need to be in our homes to feel at home. We sometimes feel that we need a reason to open our hearts: a person, a place, a time, a smell, or a taste, for example. But if we can access those feelings, those energies, through our memories and imagination, then we allow ourselves the ability to be at home and in our hearts whenever we wish.

On that afternoon day, I was stressed while preparing my things for departure. But as I realized that heart is where my home is, I realized that home travels with me. Home is not bound by any one place or person. Indeed, there is familiarity and a great need for feeling comfortable in our residences. Yet, that feeling of security is brought forth by our own ability to feel comfortable and then creating our environment as an extension of the comfort we choose to create.

After thinking these thoughts, I recognized that my heart is my traveling home. I do not wait to open my heart or feel relaxed until I return to my home now. Rather, I use my heart as the tool to create a home everywhere. The comfort that I feel in my house comes from my heart, and I can use that awareness to bring my heart out into the world. I can use my comfort to create a healing and balancing space that I carry with me, a space that is not limited to the brick and mortar that makes up the walls of my house. Indeed, the walls represent a safe place, a place where I can recharge and reopen my heart so that I can unite my heart with other things, people, and places.

Home is where the heart is because we decide it to be true. Heart is where the home is because we open its doors when we choose.

Walking Behind Truth

Following God's Will

What does it mean to walk behind truth? A simple definition might be putting God's will in front of our own will. Essentially, this means trusting that if we relax, life will still happen beautifully for us without our having to control it so tightly. So how do we walk behind truth? How can we live *from* truth?

Surrender

We most often allow ourselves to accept things mentally, but not necessarily emotionally. Surrender bridges that gap because when we are willing to accept something emotionally, we no longer push against it mentally. For example, if I can accept that I am a loving person and that I genuinely like who I am, then I will spend far less time attempting to prove that I am lovable to myself. Instead, my loving radiance will naturally be the proof that also brings about love in others.

Our mental conditioning inhibits our desire for surrender and the importance we place on it. We would rather negotiate with our mental fears so that we won't have to take that step into surrender because surrender means that we give up and accept right now as it is. It means that we put down our sword in the realization that any fighting (justifiable or not) only creates an internal fight. We have to genuinely want surrender for it to work for us. That's the beauty of it. Unless we want to put down the sword and the struggle, we will continue with mental negotiations.

Emptying Our Cup

When our cup is full of constant thoughts, we cannot receive. To fill the void that we feel inside, we try to fill up our cups with thinking, and it never creates lasting fulfillment. Instead, we need to relax so that we can empty our cup of thoughts. When we are empty in mind, we are in the best position to be filled up. The beauty is that we don't need to fill up our cups. When we stop filling our cups and create an empty space in our minds, God will fill up our cups with real substance. We can receive spiritual understanding through the calm that we create, which doesn't come from thinking, but from relaxing.

Energetic Transmutation

Energetic transmutation occurs when we allow ourselves to release, sometimes referred to as "shifting." It's what happens after we've surrendered our control over something and accepted it emotionally and permanently. We can release by crying, hugging someone, or talking it out, to list a few examples. Yet, any constructive method can be used once we're ready to release. We release by allowing ourselves to feel.

If we allow something to truly permeate us, we allow ourselves to feel the reality of it emotionally. We allow ourselves to express it and to release it. If it's anger, we allow ourselves to feel and constructively express the anger. If it's pain, we allow ourselves to feel and release the pain. In allowing ourselves to truly be there instead of covering it up with layers of thinking, we will move into the transmutation of energy much more quickly. In other words, anything that is truly embraced will lead to release and acceptance of it, whether momentarily or permanently. I've heard many teachers say that just being there to witness is enough. This is true because being there to witness means allowing ourselves to observe what is happening without judgment and feel it.

Allowing Feeling

The truth is in our feelings. When we allow our minds to be emptied and calmed, when we stop thinking, our real feelings are permitted to come up and be felt. This feeling is what I call "walking behind truth" because our feelings are our link to the truth of what's happening inside us. Thoughts point us in a direction, but feeling is at the destination where thinking has led us. If thoughts are like a train, then feelings are like the train station.

In allowing ourselves to walk behind truth, we follow what feels most truthful for us. As we follow this guidance regularly, we can establish within us a much more stabilized relationship with the continual transmutations and shifting that our spirit wants us to experience. In other words, by always saying yes to the acceptance of our experiences, we move forward. By allowing feelings to be felt, we are getting on the path that God would have us experience. Each feeling is a guide to the next experience and the next shift.

When we allow shifts to happen in us, we don't merely replace external circumstances in our lives with new ones; we change our entire realities: how we see things, how we see ourselves, and most importantly, how we feel about ourselves. In allowing ourselves to feel, we are much more likely to make permanent shifts and permanent healing. It may take days, weeks, months or longer, but ultimately, it's not up to us to determine when healing is complete. It is merely our responsibility to show up for what we are being shown and allow ourselves to feel.

Cleansing

I was coaching a friend some time ago who felt bad because she felt she should not be experiencing the things she was experiencing: crying for no reason, surfacing fears, guilt and obligations, etc. But as I related to her and explained, she began to understand that what she was allowing herself to feel was, in fact, her process of cleansing and transitioning. What was occurring in her was natural.

I explained to her that the fears and obligations she felt surfacing were not an indicator of where her life would ultimately end up. Although that conclusion is a byproduct of feeling fear, it is not true. Her feelings were merely an indicator of the cleansing process she was currently undergoing. As we discussed and pointed out some of those particulars, she accepted through her feelings of personal truth that her experience was a cleansing process. By identifying the variables within her situation, she reached the awareness she needed to relax and continue cleansing—without resistance or yielding to fear.

Since she had been conditioned her entire life that showing feeling meant weakness and that she should push her feelings down and lock them away, she had never allowed herself to release and heal her past pains fully. She was always trying to push them down instead of accepting and release them. Since she allowed herself to accept her feelings this time around, she was able to allow that natural process to continue without resistance or judgment. All I did was help her understand so that she could accept that she was going through a natural process. By eliminating the judgment of what she thought was happening and accepting it, she cleansed much more quickly and efficiently.

Feeling Better

All we need to do is feel better about things and make that our highest priority. But we each have our own way that gets us caught up in our minds. This can prevent us from feeling better and improving our situations. Sometimes, we just don't know that it's possible that we can feel better about ourselves. Sometimes, we don't have a concept of what growth and moving beyond limitations even means. But anything is possible. If we can dream it, it can happen. Thoughts are the train, remember?

Emotional Suppression

We've had so many people "should" us for so many years about what is right and what is not right for us to do when it comes to our emotions that we have become confused about what we can share. We are taught through our conditioning that emotional release is inappropriate and even that doing so equals weakness and can lead to being attacked. This kind of learned non-acceptance inhibits our ability to develop emotionally and learn how to trust ourselves and not fear our emotions.

Since our ability to trust is natural until we learn differently, we need to re-teach ourselves to do it if we want to practice healthy developmental habits. If we hide beneath layers upon layers of thinking instead of trusting, we may resort to taking a lot of unnecessary actions to promote feelings of security without truly feeling secure.

I Can Allow

The following hypothetical dialogue flows a bit differently than what you've read up until now, but it is another illustration of using tools like the Law of Attraction (the universal principle that like attracts like) to create and allow health as well as to practice what it might mean to walk behind the truth of our feelings. As in the example below, answering our own questions can lead the mind to question and reassess our actions positively. With enough practice, we find that we don't need to do or be anything other than what we are already.

"So, just being here is enough?"

"Yep."

"Don't I have to do anything?"

"Nope."

"Don't I have to teach or be an example?"

"Nope."

"Don't I need to make x amount of dollars to be successful?"

"Nope."

"Don't I have to have an opinion?"

"Nope."

"So if I can let go of what I think I should be doing, can I do what I would like to do?"

"Yes!"

"Won't that mean I won't get what I want?"

"No."

"Can I do what I love and make money at it?"

"Yes. Doing what you love is your sustenance."

"Why's that?"

"Because loving what you do puts you into alignment with who you are and thus receiving what you want. Being in alignment allows you to receive from all directions, not just the ones you designated. If you only received from the venues you planned on, you would deprive yourself of many good things when there is so much more for you to have and enjoy. You want this; you just don't know how to look for it. Being in love is how it all arrives to you."

"So why don't I allow this to happen?"

"Because you've traded feeling for thinking. For example, if I spend all my time thinking, planning, manipulating, imposing, testing, one thing is always true: I have an agenda. At the core of that agenda lies my distrust, my insecurity that all is not well and that I am not provided for. I would rather increase all of the technology that gets me the most amount of information that I need at any time and anywhere instead of trusting what I feel. Why? It's because I don't trust myself. I don't trust my feelings to guide me. So instead, I put my agenda ahead of my gut feelings. Decisions are only difficult when I have negotiated with my mind and suppressed how I felt about things. Since feelings represent my truth and my connection to my Source, in essence, I have walked ahead of truth."

"Why do I do that?"

"It's far easier to think or even borrow others' thinking than it is to trust what you feel."

"Is there something beyond thinking?"

"Yes."

"Can I get there?"

"Oh yes. You are there."

"How is that possible?"

"Because anywhere you go, you take God with you. You can't be disconnected from God; you can only forget about God being there in you. Once you leave the body, you'll remember a lot more clearly this truth."

"So what's the benefit to trying to find God/Source now?"

"Feeling the peace, love and joy of the Source that you are."

"Hmm. I wonder if I would take different actions in my life if I felt differently?"

"You would."

"How?"

"If you felt secure, you would do less to try to create security for yourself."

"That makes sense. I kind of like that. Seems like I would save a lot of time."

"You would."

"So why do I do things as I have?"

"You've been convinced that you need to."

"Are there other ways to live and still make a living?"

"Yes."

"How do I find them?"

"Imagine them."

"Then what?"

"Allow yourself to be led."

"How?"

"By listening, being calm, following the instructions given to you."

"Ohh. That means trusting my feelings again, right?"

"Yes."

"So, is there a way to know the path for me?"

"Yes. The path is already in you. It is only a matter of listening to it."

"Wow, that's deep. So to listen to the path, I just need to get quiet and empty my cup?"

"Yes, relax, find feelings that feel good, and act on them."

"What about the fearful thoughts I have?"

"Ignore them."

"But they're so convincing."

"They're unneeded."

"How do I stop them?"

"By taking your attention away from them."

"Don't I have to figure the fears out?"

"No."

"Don't I have to face fears?"

"No."

"What if I feel like I need to get past a fear to be healthy?"

"Then it will feel good for you to do so."

"What if I get depressed and I don't feel good about anything?"

"Then ask for guidance from God/Source once again. It's unlimited, and it wants you to ask unlimitedly."

"This is kind of interesting. I had no idea that being spiritual was as simple as trusting what I feel and following what I feel to be true for me."

"It is that simple, and it is highly personal. What may be true for you might not be for others."

"Won't that mean I'm wrong, or they're wrong?"

"No."

"How is that possible?"

"Because right and wrong don't even exist."

"That's not right."

"Your job is not to impose your judgments of right and

wrong. In doing so, you separate yourself from Source, and there is no truth in separation. Your job is to follow Source's plan for you by walking behind the truth of your own feelings and allowing them to teach you."

"I see. I suddenly feel like I have a lot of free time! Haha!"

"When your consciousness expands like it is doing now, you will always feel freer."

"Cool. So what can I have? What can I be and do?"

"Anything you want."

"Really?"

"Yep."

"How?"

"By asking for it and then following your feelings."

"What if it doesn't show up right away?"

"It is not your job to manage how or when things show up. It is only your job to manage you."

"What does that mean?"

"It means it is your responsibility to manage how you feel so that you can be in alignment with what you want."

"What does 'alignment' mean?"

"It means that if the thought of something you want *feels* good, then it will be most important to *keep feeling good*."

"Oh. So how do I feel good if I don't have what I want?"

"You pretend that you do have it. Appreciate what you have. Anything can be used to feel good, and it will work the same."

"Cool! You know, I'm starting to feel better just focusing my attention on this stuff."

"That's good."

"Why do I feel better?"

"Because you are focusing your attention on your feelings, and in following your feelings, you are following your truth."

"Interesting. I'll have to contemplate that."

"Feel free to."

How to Trust Your Guidance

The Priority of Willingness

When we choose to surrender control, we choose to practice willingness. Willingness means we are open to receive and to serve. It means we are making our alignment with God our top priority. No matter where we stand, there are always positive steps that we can take that are right in front of us, which will create alignment within us: exercise, eating healthy food, etc. When we do take these steps, we feel better. As we take a step, we are given another step. It's easy, but we don't always make it easy. Our willingness determines if we think and do the things that make us feel better. If we're not willing to feel better, then we're not that serious about making improvements in our life.

Are You Serious?

The only reason we want anything is that we think we'll feel better after having it. But if we're not serious about feeling better, if our desire is merely a fleeting and impulsive want which we believe is an insurmountable obstacle or an impossible task, then it will remain a want. But is it a want, or is it a decision?

Doing God's Work

When we make alignment (feeling better) our top priority, we are putting ourselves in a position to receive. When we choose this, we are doing what God wants us to do because feeling good is feeling God. Feeling God is feeling alignment. Doing God's work means doing work that feels good to do. Doing God's work puts us into alignment with everything else in our lives. We perform our work with better quality, accuracy and attitude. We have more positive interactions with others. Making 'feeling better' our top priority aligns us with receiving better things.

Feel Good Nudges

Following a choice that feels better may sometimes peel us away from what we intend to work on, like writing a book, for example. In this sense, it may seem extremely counterproductive to follow a feel-good impulse or nudge to eat at a restaurant when we have a book that we feel we must be writing instead. But the choice to trust our guidance means that we choose to follow our feel-good impulses over our agendas. Trusting these feel-good impulses despite our ego's compulsive agenda tells us that we are choosing alignment. A dead giveaway of compulsive ego agenda is that there is nothing in it that feels good or asks us to trust. Ego only promises that we will feel good but rarely delivers.

Releasing Expectations

When our desires are truly heartfelt and not based on impulsive want, we can afford to trust our guidance to surrender our control over more things. We trust our guidance when we realize that our choice to follow a better-feeling action has provided us with a higher quality experience, even if it doesn't yield an anticipated result. Choosing to follow good feeling nudges despite the need to foresee an anticipated result is the birth of surrender. When we give up our expectations, we can follow the better feeling action without agenda. Therefore, we are trusting our guidance. If the only time we can feel good is when we've accomplished some ego goal, we can be sure that the following 'feel-good' will be short-lived. Not only that, depending on the length of the goal's project, it can be a long time until the next time ego allows us to feel good. There's no freedom in compulsive accomplishment because it chokes out joy in the process. The destination is enjoying the journey.

Joyful Agenda

God manages the real agendas of our lives, and if we are not allowing Him to manage our lives, most, if not all, of our efforts will feel empty or short-lived. You might say, "But I'm not getting things done!" The things we need to get done will always be there for us, and we will never cross everything off of our list to get done. There will always be something more for us to do. In that sense, it doesn't matter what we get accomplished. Our goal isn't to get it all done but to do it joyfully and to do it because it feels good as we do it. We don't need agendas to feel joy. We need joy to carry out the agendas.

Granted, we have bills to pay. But unless we are paying a bill at the last second, let's step away and find a way to feel better, get into alignment and then come back to pay our bills. The simple practice of feeling better before acting in application to anything will save more time in our spiritual growth than we might think.

Graceful Living

A most graceful way to live life is to trust the feel-good steps we take to create positive results in our life. This isn't to be confused with overindulgence or self-medication. It means making it a priority to find a way to feel good while doing any task, if only in a simple, positive thought. The results will astound us.

Our trust keeps us connected to the ever-flowing stream of God's guidance and feeling good. Our level of success is measured by our love, peace and joy and depends on our willingness to choose the thoughts or feelings that feel better. Our guidance will deepen with practice, and we will internally graduate to higher levels of being. Through living from aligned feelings, we will always be in the right place at the right time. When our priority is listening to our feelings, we will be undisturbed by appearances and trust even more. By checking in with our feelings and being honest with ourselves about what we are feeling, we put God first. This is living in Grace.

Healthy Boundaries

Guardian Angel's Guide to Dealing With Challenging People

Changing Times, Changing Minds

You'll need to develop an entirely new skill set for working with people in today's world. In your newly emerging consciousness, you are opening yourself to another realm of possibilities, one through which you will be shining your light into new places and sharing your consciousness with new people.

Challenging People

Perhaps the vibe you feel from someone (we'll call him John) seems to be somewhat intrusive. Maybe John is behaving in a manner that feels irritable to you. Whichever the case, you would normally let it roll off your shoulders. Today things feel different, however.

You may be feeling that everything you try doesn't work with this issue. This may lead to a bit of inner panic or a 'fight or flight' mechanism without making the true cause of discomfort known to you. So each attempt that appears to be unsuccessful reinforces the notion that something outside of you has power over you. One of the gold nuggets here is to take a step away from the internal resistant programming currently operating within you. Stepping away affords you the choice for more freedom when you feel you have little or no control or options.

Gold Nugget

If you can get to the point of acknowledging that *you are in the process of creating a solution* to your problem, you are internally overcoming the problem by your acceptance of its presence. By doing this, you are reaffirming to your mind that there is a real solution (which there always is) instead of falling victim to the resistant programming that has arisen, which says, "you're not going to make it through this."

Perhaps you dismiss your instincts as irrational because you cannot validate or justify your feelings enough to make a positive confrontation with John. Nevertheless, this does not mean that you cannot follow and trust your feelings. You still can! You can use your feelings to guide you through this period of uncertainty and into a positive solution that will ultimately benefit how you interact in all relationships, including the one with John.

It's Not You; It's Me

The most important thing to recognize when someone causes resistance, fear, or a negative reaction is that it is happening inside you. You are feeling it. You own it. Whether it's something they did to you or didn't do to you, if you are feeling it, it is a part of your own experience. If you can admit that, then you've taken your first step into resolving your problem—you've accepted that it's there. Accepting that something feels bad in your feelings is a huge step forward in taking spiritual responsibility. Remember, life is an emotional journey, and the more you manage how you feel, the less time you will be spending trying to manage others.

It's Still Not You; It's Me

The second most important thing to remember when you feel a negative reaction is that you do not need other people to resolve the negative feeling. You do not need to change a person or situation to create change. When you change how you feel inside, situations will begin to change along with you on the outside. Many times, a new perspective is all that is needed to completely change how you participate in life.

Patience

Since you've accepted the fact that you are feeling negative, you are halfway to overcoming it. Now, you have afforded yourself the ability to be patient. Acknowledge to yourself that you haven't yet arrived at the place where you want to be in your feelings, and realize that you are giving yourself permission to take some time to figure and feel it all out. The issue isn't going anywhere without you because it is inside of you. Take all the time you need. Take a breath.

The overall objective here is to look inside when you get upset instead of looking outside. Blame is almost inevitable when you look outside of yourself while being upset. The feelings of discomfort that come with negative interactions are why people do not deal with other people and themselves more constructively. But you have the power to change your feelings. You are more than your reactive patterns. Maybe no one's told you that, but it's true. With a little patience and breathing room, you can allow yourself the space you need to deal with this issue internally. By doing so, you are improving your psychological conditioning and approach to all social situations.

Resistance is not Strength

Resistance is not strength, although it disguises itself that way. For example, when a person witnesses forcefulness, they witnesses powerlessness. The amount of forcefulness (or control) a person exhibits is strangely similar to the amount of powerlessness they feel inside. The reason a person misperceives their resistance as strength is because being forceful helps them achieve desired results. But the mere fact that being forceful occasionally yields favorable results in no way teaches true power. Resistance teaches false power.

Resistance (or non-acceptance) of another person's behavior may masquerade as inappropriate behavior. While John may be exhibiting inappropriate behavior by most people's standards, upon exploring the issue further, you may find that what you do not accept about John's behavior is the smokescreen of your ego attempting to hide your reactive conditioning from you by directing it at someone else. Your ego doesn't want you to know that your problem with John is your problem (but it is), and you can't fix how you relate with John by retaliating his behavior. Doing so may offer you a temporary form of relief, but more than likely at some long-term expense.

Releasing Resistance

One of the best things you can do with resistance is accept that you are uncomfortable or annoyed. In doing so, you immediately introduce acceptance. You will find that the door to releasing the resistance begins to open slowly. Accepting your discomfort will feel like a relief, serving as an emotional release and giving you a sense of freedom. By accepting your resistance, you will learn that the situation or person did not need to change, but something in you did. As you choose to release the resistance, you are moving forward into acceptance. In realizing this, you will discover that making the management and release of your emotions a priority also helps you release situations and people—and most of all—yourself.

Wisdom from Resistance

Remember that all pain is temporary, and no matter how temporarily painful a problem is, the amount of pain or resistance you feel during a problem is usually related to how much you believe that you don't have control in that situation for that moment. Thereby, issues tend to represent, symbolize and even simulate things more than they point out facts about what you perceive outside of you. The trick is not to let your temporarily painful experience get in the way of when you constructively address it.

Take your time with this. It doesn't get mastered by understanding it, but understanding can be a doorway into acceptance in your experience. Take time to be with your feelings. Experience them. Trust what you feel. Layers of resistance cover your true feelings, so you'll have to allow yourself to experience the emotion that the resistance is protecting if you want to learn the truth of its presence. If you're willing to do that, you will maximize your growth opportunity of the emotion arising within you in the first place.

These things are presented as points of exploration to help you. Remember to take your time. Remember to be kind and patient with yourself. Life will go on. I'm here for you.

—Your Guardian Angel

Don't Should on Me

Should Equals Guilt

No matter how we look at it, "should" means "guilt." Guilt means non-acceptance of self. Guilt means whatever the ego or darkness would have us believe about ourselves instead of the beautiful light we truly are. We are perfect as God's creation.

So why even have the "shoulding?" We each have light and dark in us. That's not bad; it's just how we're made. We exist in a world born of separation, so all of us beings in it would be subject to the same contrast.

Pulling Splinters

The light in us is what we are—the God, the Source. The darkness in us is unreal. The great thing is that the darkness does not come with us when we die. It's only an illusion. The light in us stays and grows. Isn't that wonderful?

The real challenge is learning how to consciously choose to play only in the light and renounce all seduction of the darkness. This does not mean to fear the darkness but rather to accept it. Acceptance of fear transmutes its influence. Since we have many fears embedded in us, it is important to nurture the release of those fears, but only when we feel the timing is right. If I have a splinter in my finger, I wouldn't want to pull it out before it's ready. I might end up gouging my skin and bleeding. If I allow nature to take its course, however—if I don't resist—it will push itself out in its own time.

Succumbing to Fear

Okay, so back to "shoulding." We "should" on ourselves quite a bit. This is the guilt in us, the ego and the pain in us. Guilt is the stuff that begs us to succumb to it and stay in illusion and bondage with ourselves. When we are "shoulding" ourselves, we are succumbing to fear. The actions we take when we feel we should do something are almost always based on fear; fear of what others think of us, fear of ourselves, fear of shining our light, fear of being seen for who we are, fear for being seen for anything other than what our egos want us to be seen for. We even should on ourselves spiritually!

Ego "Shoulds" Me

I've always strived to do my best with everything, but that doesn't mean that I've always succeeded. I've had plenty of failures. But just as I believe an error doesn't become a mistake until I refuse to correct it, I also believe that an undesirable result (deemed as a failure) doesn't become an ego identity until I choose to believe that my success as a person solely comes from what I do in the world. That got me thinking more about the ego's antics which made me believe in failure in the first place.

Even now, I still have fears of failure. But I am not jailed by those fears as I once had been. My usual strategy in growing up and dealing with the ego that hid within me was to "do my best." Doing my best meant that I gave my best effort. But "efforting" meant that if I was not giving my best, then I felt I was not good enough as an individual. The result is that I ended up shoulding myself into overexertion while teaching myself that effort equaled my worth. Guess what the result was? I only allowed me to experience myself in one particular way, and it is in this way that my ego had approved my "should-hood."

In trying to be a better person, I have learned that my ego tells me that I am only valuable if I am doing something nice for someone else, and if I am not, then I "should" be doing something about it. That guilty feeling tells me that I won't feel comfortable unless I am doing something for someone else or having my value recognized by someone else. This feeling guilty is the ego, and it is easy to see that ego has infiltrated my social conditioning. The more guilt I have had, the more I have felt obligated to do things for other people because I've been afraid of how I might be perceived otherwise. Without becoming aware of ego's guilt tactics operating inside of me, giving me that gut-wrenching feeling, I would have remained a pawn to ego's guilt as well as the guilt operating in everyone else!

Freedom from "Shoulds"

I once was afraid of being seen as anything other than a "good" person. This is fear of guilt (and the birth of obligation). I was also afraid of not being accepted. Most of what I shared of myself was based on how *I anticipated I'd be perceived*. My desire to serve others was sincere, yet I also had my wounds to heal like anyone else. All of my Source energy was being pushed through a little hourglass until fear bottlenecked it in the middle.

I had a lot to give, but my fears constrained my expression. There was so much more of me that I needed to express, but I didn't know any better way to do so than through the means which I had already learned. When my need for expansion grew to the point of no return, I broke through the hourglass, and great energies flowed. Then, it became far easier to let go of things like worrying about what others thought of me, pleasing others, and so forth. The result of letting myself be limitless by releasing my shoulds was freedom. Our spirits love freedom.

Does it take courage? It does. But it's worthwhile, and letting go of things (surrendering, forgiving) that limit us is never something we regret. It's not always something we know how to do, either. It takes years of practice and trials and errors with years of layered conditioning to peel away. Yet each layer blossoms gifts that we would have normally suppressed by staying in the bottlenecked hourglass. This is a lot of what having a spiritual path means. It's about releasing layers of what isn't needed, which is the most liberating thing when we're ready because we gain more freedom every time we choose it.

Roles and Identities

I'm a teacher, chef or parent. Unfortunately, we take on these identities and become so accustomed to our roles that we forget we are more than those roles. Although valuable when used in service and as a form of spiritual expression, roles can also become tools of the ego. Some tell-tale signs of when the ego has taken control of us might be when we are afraid of losing a role, a person, or how we're being perceived. Having a good reputation is nice, but it's detrimental if the role or identity creates that bottlenecking hourglass of spiritual stagnation.

Of course, we are perfect and lovable as we are, and there is nothing wrong with the wonderful ways we serve. Only the ego would have us defend what we do or attach to what we do. It's only the ego that would have us limit our expression of ourselves. This is where the Self-shoulding comes in again. We should ourselves up and down the sidewalk every day. Sometimes, we don't even feel the shoulds at a conscious level, yet we act them out through conditioning. So how do we get around all the shoulding?

A great thing to do is recognize those moments when we feel like there is something inside of us trying to compete with us. Under that should, we can detect in our feelings how there might be a bit of pain, fear or discomfort. We may not feel guilty, per se, but all negative and guilty feelings point back to fear. We don't want to succumb to it. Instead of succumbing to the fear, let's step back and take a deep breath.

The "Should" Disguise

Shoulding disguises itself as "the right thing to do." If we feel like what we're doing is the right thing to do, then it is. If we don't feel right about doing something, we're shoulding ourselves or not being true to our feelings. The right thing to do is generally a collective agreement among a culture of people. Spiritually speaking, however, the right thing to do is best answered by us as individuals as doing what most aligns with our feelings of guidance and goodness. Anything less is a disguise.

Obligation and social conditioning are among the most prevalent inducers of disguising ourselves, often for the sake of keeping up appearances. With obligation, it's not so much "what if I do it?" as it is "what if I don't do it?" or "what will I personally lose if I don't do it?" These questions induce guilt-laden responses. "What will they think of me if I don't respond the way they expect me to respond?"

Should is a double-edged sword because it can strengthen the identities of our social groups via guilt, regret and obligation while at the same time suppress us as individuals. Anything that causes guilt also cuts us off from our freedom. Ironically, a group designed for harmony may be held together by the illusion of harmony, with guilt as its framework for peace-keeping.

If we did what we felt was the right thing to do on the inside, instead of what was the right thing to do in others' eyes, then we might be perceived differently, not understood, or maybe even judged by others. But the fear of being judged by others is yet again our ego judging us.

An overwhelming thought, perhaps? It doesn't have to be. The light also abounds, and it shines through each of us every day. Yes, love is real, God is real, and it's all happening in us all the time. There is only power in the light and none in darkness. Our simple awareness of ourselves helps us and all of humanity. Every bit of love that we choose to acknowledge and see changes things. And if we see ourselves shoulding, it's in our best interest to step back, breathe, and ask Source for instructions.

Expression as Salvation

I believe the expression of who I am to be a key to my salvation. If we have the courage to express ourselves, we'll be in much better alignment with everything about us: our health, other people, our happiness, our Source. The question is: which do we choose when faced with the choice to should or the choice to express? Should means suppressing or doing something that we are expected to do.

Express means doing something that is in our heart and feelings to do right now. Sometimes the need to express may be a glimmer, and other times, it may be a screaming, burning necessity. Sometimes, we just can't hold it in any longer. And what happens? We explode! We must release. Energy must move through us. We must be allowed to express ourselves somehow, some way; otherwise, we will develop misalignment.

"I AM" or "AM I?"

God is about allowing ourselves to be used by Him. It's about allowing Source to be felt and to be with us. Trusting God in this way may or may not be understood by other people. It comes down to us being honest with ourselves. Is it I AM, or is it AM I? Are we allowing the God in us to lead us down the path He would have us walk? It feels so good when we do! Or are we allowing should to lead us down the path of resistance because we can't surmount the fears? Our thoughts may be used for making more conscious decisions that lead each of us into love, peace and acceptance. Acceptance of ourselves is what naturally creates peace. When we eliminate should, we create self-acceptance.

Sometimes when I'm driving on the road, I look over at the driver next to me. I can't help but wonder what's happening in their consciousness. Where do they want to drive? Why are they going there? To feel better? Because they feel they should? Or are they all happy as God would have them be? What is driving that car at that moment? Love or fear?

Turning "Should" Around

We have the permission to ask ourselves questions about what doesn't feel good to us. We are allowed to find ways to feel better about anything. Perhaps we haven't discovered a new way to feel about things? Let's turn should around, shall we? Let's use should in a new way that promotes our power to choose instead of in the old way that should steals our power.

Let's try some fun examples: Should I be working this job? Or, can I imagine myself feeling better doing something new? Should I be in this relationship? Or, can I imagine myself feeling better being alone or with someone else? Should I live in this town? Or, can I imagine myself feeling better if I lived somewhere else? Should I be listening to this person? Or, can I imagine myself feeling better listening to myself or someone else?

Do the answers resemble what we haven't yet *allowed* ourselves to have? Has should stopped us from having what we want? When we begin reframing the guilt-inducing questions we ask ourselves that begin with should to empowering questions, we promote our freedom. Also, when we stop listening to sentences spoken to us that begin with "You should…," we automatically get back onto the path of allowing. Imagining the possibilities helps us to create the change we want to see.

Creating Positive Change

Asking ourselves questions jogs our minds out of routine thinking and helps us discover where our limitations reside within us. This practice can show us where change may be needed in our lives even if we did not consider or realize that change was possible. When we pose questions to ourselves, we need to be as honest as possible in answering them. Practicing self-honesty in our answers can mean the difference between taking definite, healthy and needed steps forward instead of rationalizing, not changing and then convincing ourselves that the rationalization is a spiritual choice.

With every single day, with every choice we make, we can turn inward and feel and begin to allow. The end of shoulding is the beginning of allowing. We don't have to live with should as the substitute for our true passions. We can move beyond that—one should at a time—creating the awareness that offers us freedom.

Compassionate Detachment

An old saying tells us that two people who are close friends or lovers are "attached at the hip." So why would we want to detach from them at all? Wouldn't we want to stay close to the people that we love the most? A whole new meaning evolves once we combine the seemingly contradictory words compassion and detachment.

The Argument

Before we talk about why we might detach from someone, let's talk about what happens when attached to someone. Let's say that Jane invited John to dinner and served him something that he had told her more than once in the past he didn't like eating. John became offended, thinking that Jane wasn't showing enough consideration for John by remembering that he didn't like eating asparagus. Then, Jane became offended because she remembered that John had criticized her cooking in the past. They start arguing about cooking quality and about showing respect for people's eating preferences.

Jane and John are both upset and projecting words and feelings charged with energy and beliefs, thought processes, attitudes, judgments, expectations, pain, and more. So it is no wonder that they don't understand each other. They are too caught up in their projections.

In an argument, it can be easy to see these things occurring if we are observing from a detached perspective. We use the example of an argument because it is an example of energy clashing between two people, and we can feel this energy strongly. After observing some of these dynamics, you might say that, during an argument, we are energetically attached.

Our Projections

If we are energetically attached, how do we then detach? First of all, we don't need to take offense. Given this, it can be challenging not to be offended during an argument. But that doesn't mean we can't learn how to do it! When we take offense, we are reacting to what someone says. But who are we truly reacting to? The answer is our self. The person with whom we are arguing will mirror back to us whatever we have inside of us, or more specifically, whatever we are projecting at them. To put it another way, whatever we think others have going on inside of them is going on inside of us first. We have to be feeling it for ourselves before we can project our perception onto someone else. This gives us the opportunity to take responsibility in a way that we may have never done before. This approach lets us know that our projections are the cause of our negativity and not others. Even if another person is causing trouble for us, the responsibility we can take empowers us to remain unattached to their drama and stay in our power.

During our day, we notice arguments on television, in the workplace and more. But we are not involved with them. We are merely observers. It's easy to remain detached when we are not involved. Yet, we can still be energetically detached while we are involved! If we keep in mind that what people

83

say to us comes from them—their attitudes, beliefs, and expectations—we can remember that what they say has little to do with us. How well could we detach while in an argument if we knew that the one arguing with us was only saying something about him? Even if what he says is about you, it is still a projection coming from him. It is his creation. It is his interpretation of you, and that is not who you are.

When we get upset and attach to what is happening around us, we begin to lose ourselves in what is happening. We may become irate and lose control, or we may experience minor irritation. Either way, we begin to feel negative and perhaps even defensive, and when we allow ourselves to attach like that, we lose clarity and objectivity.

Fueling Our Projections

Let's say I am driving to work, and someone in another car does something reckless. Maybe they pass by in front of me at a dangerous speed and cut me off. I attach to the situation and become angry. I wave my fist and yell at them because I feel justified in expressing my anger. Yet, I arrive at work, and an hour later, I am still fanning the flames of my anger. I enable the past situation to recharge my anger by alternating between my feelings of anger and my thoughts about it. I am making my negativity stronger. I am talking about it with co-workers, rallying them to become angry and upset with me to feel further justified in my anger.

This example illustrates that I am not clear and centered because I am fueling my anger. I am attached to the drama. I call this having an "energetic blockage." Blockages are denser energies like anger and fear that cut off that natural flow of positive energy in us. Blockages inhibit our ability to see the outside world.

What if the person in the opposing vehicle was speeding to get to a hospital to see his dying son? Or what if the person who came into our lane without signaling was an old lady who just got her license renewed but is a little forgetful? In these cases, we attached to the drama by creating anger, but we wouldn't have judged them had we known the whole story. Instead, we might have had compassion.

When we teach ourselves how to remain detached, we take ultimate responsibility for our emotions. The more we practice compassionate detachment, the more we can see clearly. We begin to perceive without judgment and expectation. We begin seeing everything around us more clearly because we are no longer only seeing what we are projecting. When we choose to perceive differently, when we choose to acknowledge that there is a larger story than what we can see, we may begin to choose to be more responsible with what we perceive and project as a result.

We sometimes become confused because we forget the difference between creating projections and perceiving what is happening. We see through our subjective lens so often that we forget that there is a world beyond the way that we interpret it. In the driving example, it is clear that I responded to the situation by creating a block (upset) in my energy. Since energy always flows and must be eventually released, the blockages inside me will seek release, and I will subconsciously create opportunities to unblock that flow. Those opportunities will likely manifest into my experience as obstacles, challenges and things that don't appear to be going my way.

Expectation

There is more to the world than how we perceive and understand it, and we are the only force stopping ourselves from seeing more of it. When we detach and no longer project our expectations about the world or the people in it, we will feel better. In our willingness to see things differently, we permit ourselves to see with much more clarity. One of the most important gifts we give ourselves is the opportunity to see clearly who we are, and we achieve this through awareness.

If I had an expectation that you respond to me in a certain way and you respond differently than I expect you to, then I may become upset because you didn't respond how I wanted you to respond. My expectation is my projection. It is my attempt to control your behavior. Since my expectation is not your expectation, you are most likely not upset with my behavior. How could you be upset? You have no idea what I am feeling inside of me. My projection is a game that I play with myself, even though I pretend that you are playing the game with me. In the end, I made myself upset because I projected expectations which I placed upon you, and you were probably unaware that it even happened.

On the other hand, if I release my expectation that you should respond to me in a certain way, I am no longer giving you the power to make me emotionally upset. That means that if I make my happiness somehow dependent upon you, then I am placing my happiness in your hands. If my happiness is based on an external condition, I won't be happy unless that external condition is making me happy.

We can even take this a step further. Not only can we not expect externals to make us happy, but we also discover that

86

nothing set in time can make us happy. Our happiness only comes from what we experience in this moment. If I am living in this moment and not placing an expectation upon a person, the world, or anything external, then I am free to be happy. When I give up my expectations, when I let people off the hook, I am free and detached to love in this moment for what the moment offers.

Let's say we have released all of our expectations and have detached from the world around us. We still love the world and the people in it. However, we are no longer subject to its influence. We are now at the point where we can love the world without allowing its drama to become our drama. We can now compassionately detach from family and friends. This allows us to love those around us without enabling their dramas. This is compassionately detaching.

Unconscious Feeding

There is a story about a boy who traveled in a hot air balloon. He came across a meadow where he saw another boy on a farm who had fallen in the mud and was stuck. The boy in the balloon was happy he could help and flew over to the boy in the mud and threw down a rope. The stuck boy began to pull the rope. The boy in the balloon noticed that the boy in the mud was not getting free from the mud. Not only that, he noticed that the boy was so stuck in the mud that he was pulling the balloon down to the ground. The boy in the balloon cried out to the boy in the mud that his balloon was not strong enough to pull him out of the mud and that he needed to let go of the rope. The boy stuck in the mud was too distracted by his dilemma to notice that he was pulling the boy and the balloon to the ground. Eventually, the two boys and the hot air balloon were stuck in the mud.

The boy in the mud was too busy living out his unconscious drama to be aware that he was pulling another person into it. He may have wanted to get out of the mud at an unconscious level, but he did not have enough awareness to know that he was hurting someone else in the process. In addition, what the balloon story did not reveal was that the boy in the mud was afraid of heights.

A person might be more comfortable in the mud than facing the prospect of climbing the rope to freedom. Given options, people tend to make the less fearful choice. If we are looking from the vantage point of the person in the mud, when we see someone flying by in a hot air balloon with a rope, we may be attracted to the freedom that they seem to have, but we may not be ready to lift ourselves out of the mud and up to that level. Because, sometimes, we only want to feel a little bit better but not feel good enough to get unstuck.

If a person we are trying to help is in a deeply unconscious state, they cannot recognize the difference between feeding off of our energy versus becoming conscious. Feeding occurs when a person sucks our energy out of us while we help them, but they still want to stay stuck in the mud because the mud is familiar even though it is unhealthy. Becoming conscious occurs when a person we help chooses to get unstuck from the mud and is aware enough to know what is and is not harmful to the person helping them.

Each of us needs to be aware of whether or not helping someone else sinks our balloon and enables them to feed on us. It is not appropriate for us to help someone if it puts our health at risk. If it does, it may be time to decline their call for help, refer them to someone else, release the relationship, or seek a qualified professional.

Feeding happens when we steal other people's energy. Feeding gives a false fix or a temporary relief to a problem without healing it. Feeding makes our plight feel temporarily better, but the problem remains. When we are ready to give up feeding, we are ready to go inward to our Source-led feelings for true security and guidance instead of relying on someone else to feel better. Examples of feeding are manipulating and controlling, taking advantage of others, gossiping and complaining, or anything negative which creates separation. Feeding is the seduction of our consciousness led away from Source. In feeding, we are afraid to trust ourselves. Instead, we need to steal energy from others, and we need others to feel better about ourselves.

As we detach from the feeding in our life, our example can encourage others to detach from the feeding in their own life. If people value their feeding more than they value our help, they will find someone else who will enable their feeding. It is a tremendous act of self-love and courage to not engage in the feeding and the drama of others because it may mean that we lose those relationships or that they may change. If we lose them, our relationship with them can transform and evolve, or it may be replaced with new relationships that sustain our healthy choices. Detaching from feeding isn't an excuse to be arrogant. On the contrary, it is an opportunity to practice wiser love, better health and compassionate detachment.

Relationships

When People Don't Smile

Social Awkwardness

Have you ever felt afraid of how you might be perceived if you smiled and said hello to someone you didn't know? Or they didn't return your smile?

In most cases, it's not an insult when people don't smile back. I've come to learn that we tend not to smile when we are uncomfortable. But, ironically, we also smile and laugh when we feel uncomfortable to cover up our discomfort.

When we venture into the public, we collectively agree when it is appropriate to smile, say thank you, or even not smile. A forgiving smile in traffic might be misinterpreted and returned to you as a choice display of fingers. We don't always know when to smile, so we rely on our conditioning to tell us how to act while experiencing as little discomfort as possible.

Smiling Connects Us with Others

The simplest sign of acceptance is a smile. Through language barriers or the inability to find the words to relate, we can still show acceptance through our smiles. We can use a smile to create unification, confidence, courage, and connectivity. Smiling is a show of strength, not weakness. It is a sign of confidence, openness, friendliness, approachability and self-worth. Those deer in the headlights faces are faces of discomfort. Don't be fooled or dissuaded by stoic, non-smiling faces. It often means that a particular smile is afraid to show itself.

A smile is profoundly valuable in situations we find to be unfamiliar or uncomfortable. I don't mean that we should laugh nervously and uncontrollably or smile because we're uncomfortable or show dominance. I mean to offer a smile through your courage even when you don't know if you'll get a smile in return. A smile of initiation is a confident, courageous effort that invites a smile in return.

Smiling Small Talk

You can use a smile and a "Hiya doin'?" to easily strike up a conversation. Most folks become much more comfortable with people they don't know if they can engage in some small talk, like weather or sports. Yet this comes with some caution.

Warning: Use small talk sparingly. Not for use in real relationship building. Discontinue use and flush thoroughly with water if irritation continues. Move on to something else once rapport is established to avoid stagnancy.

Using small talk can bridge the gap with people you aren't familiar with or with people you might normally have little to say. Your mind may tell you that there's no reason to speak. Ignore it. Your smile can see beyond your mind's reach.

Smiling Reduces Threat

For the non-smiling mind to lower its defenses, it requires

sameness; similar interests, similar looks, similar jobs, or anything similar. Similarities are the most non-threatening things to non-smiling minds. But if a heart connection is made through a smile and a look in their eyes, all of those mental filters aren't needed. The mental filters are merely a way for the brain to assess a possible threat. Therefore, people we regularly smile at are not necessarily friends, but people we've decided are nonthreatening.

Smiling Promotes Acceptance

Smiling does not necessarily mean that our hearts are open. For some, smiling is a tool used by the mind to qualify whether or not acceptance is possible or even a priority. The non-smiling mind wants to ask the question to everyone it encounters, *"Is this person similar to me, or different?"* A smile traverses this boundary and promotes consciousness growth by bypassing the mind's subject-object orientation. When people feel that you won't attack them, they will warm up to you.

Smile Before Thinking

When we seek to connect with others, no matter what's going on, we can project acceptance through a smile without having to analyze the situation or guess whether or not we'll be accepted. Being the first one to smile *is* a show of self-acceptance. We don't have to figure our way into someone else's acceptance of us or attempt to win them over. Our smiling will naturally make people want to lower their guard and feel comfortable. Smiling shows that we are comfortable with ourselves.

Smiles Heal

With great smiles comes great healing. Giving a simple smile away may induce a feeling of compassion, nurturing and healing in another person. When we are willing to smile at the right moment, it can prevent emotional turmoil, turn anger away and dry tears.

Smiles Induce Chemistry

If we feel a genuine smile coming from a person that we are being introduced to or even a stranger at our gym who we regularly encounter, we feel more open around that person. We even perceive them as friendly and non-threatening. Even if we have no chemistry with someone we speak with without smiling, I can assure you that they will believe there is chemistry between you with a returned smile. Why is this? It is because there is always chemistry in the heart.

Smile First

Smile first. Smile hard. Smile with all of your elbow grease. A smile is the simplest doorway into acceptance. No need to think or analyze; look into their eyes and shine your smile and those who are ready will smile back.

The Bug Lady

Looking for God

In any relationship, it can be easy for us to prejudge a situation or person. For example, we want to judge books by their covers because it is easier to make a quick judgment from the outside looking in than skimming through the many chapters in each book to determine whether or not we want to buy the book. We do the same thing with people. We constantly evaluate and choose how deeply we want to look into others. Do we judge them at face value alone, or do we invest our time looking for the God in them?

Looking for the God in others can be especially difficult when they behave negatively. They give us no incentive to be compassionate with them. It's a lot easier to be compassionate to positive, open people rather than negative, closed-off people. When someone is behaving negatively towards us, it is always an invitation to us, first and foremost, to practice our defenselessness. By that, I mean doing the things that keep us centered and connected to Source. We can maintain our spiritual connection by meditating, reading scripture or (my favorite) prayer so that we are ready to put our growth into practice when these situations arise.

Defenselessness

As we maintain our spiritual connection, we are more defenseless. We are strong. We feel no inclination to attack others because, in our defenselessness, we do not attack ourselves. We can't condemn others if we are not already first condemning ourselves. From this state of defenselessness, not only do we feel peaceful, but we can also remain compassionate to the defenses of others. Maintaining this attitude helps us to flood compassion into the world with tremendous magnitude and power. With our focus on offering no defense, we do not resist others' defenses. We are safe from attacking ourselves and others. Being a friend to ourselves, we are everyone's friend. My story about the bug lady illustrates this.

The Bug Lady

When I had an insect problem in my house, my landlord put me in touch with his exterminator. My roommate had spoken with the bug lady briefly and had warned me that she was somewhat abrasive on the phone. Because my roommate would be out of town, I would have to deal with the bug lady entirely on my own.

When the bug lady first called me for an appointment, she insisted that I write our meeting time down, but since I was in my vehicle at the time, I wasn't able to write. Although she wasn't rude, she didn't take my word that I would remember the appointment. I interpreted her disbelief and slight abrasiveness as being jaded by past clients' failure to remember their appointments with her. I am also convinced, however, that people don't come out of the womb pissed off.

I was not looking forward to the appointment, and I prayed that it would go smoothly. I intended that the encounter went well when she came over to the house in two weeks to spray for bugs.

The day came, and Logan (my Labrador Retriever) and I were out for an early morning walk. I had good, prayerful conversations with God during the walk. When I returned, the bug lady was waiting for me a half-hour earlier than our appointed time. The first thing she said to me when she exited her vehicle (other than verifying that I was the guy with the bug problem), was, "I didn't think you would show up," in a thick-skinned manner. That aggravated me at that time because few things were more annoying to me than antagonists who insisted on starting their interactions negatively, much like spending months building an ocean liner and right before its maiden voyage drilling a hole in the shiny new hull. We may have had high aspirations for the ship's first encounter with the sea, but our effort was self-defeating from the start.

As she came into my house, I did my best to stay centered and defenseless, careful not to misinterpret her abrasiveness as negativity. I truly felt that underneath her thick skin, her aim was not to attack me. It felt more to me like the world jaded her. A great exercise that I had practiced during that time was treating someone I did not feel natural chemistry with like they were a close friend or even imagining hugging them. This always seemed to help me feel closer and more open with a personality whom my mind was not accustomed to being open.

Removing Defenses

As she requested, I moved things away from the window sills so she could spray insecticide. In the course of our time together, she seemed to open up a bit more. All I can say with certainty was that I was willing to help her however I could and that I wasn't returning any of what I considered to be negative energy. I can only speculate as to why she continued to open up as much as she did. Still, I believe that her defenses came down without any negativity being perpetuated by either of us.

She was probably used to people not showing up for her, having high expectations of her, or being upset and stressed because whenever she'd see a customer, it was because they had a problem, and she stood between the customer and the solution. I can only imagine how much stress continual demands might accumulate with her business in insect extermination. I also felt that my choice to acknowledge these things, which gave her the benefit of the doubt, helped me open my heart to her, disarming my own defenses, even though I wasn't sharing my thoughts aloud.

Opening Up

Shortly after that, the things she was saying no longer had the tone of "you should do this and this or else this will happen," but changed to the tone of "this is a really good idea to do this because…." Her eye contact with me increased, and she even returned my smiles in acknowledging what she was sharing. Since I had chosen to lower my defenses, it was easy for me to come from compassion. I began feeling more intense the need to give her every opportunity to feel better about our interaction. I felt that she truly needed to have a positive experience with someone who appreciated what she was offering instead of making demands. I focused on listening to her when she spoke, paraphrased and asked questions and held good eye contact. I never retaliated when there were thick-skinned comments like there were at the beginning. My broadcast was calm. Our whole meeting lasted no more than twenty minutes.

I couldn't have told you ahead of time that the encounter would go that positively. I only knew that I was determined not to give back the negativity I initially felt I received, and in doing so, I prevented myself from becoming defensive in return. So, in essence, my desire to stop her negativity ironically became an effort to stop my negativity. After all, my button for pain was activated in the first place, which brought about the need for me to act differently in this encounter.

The Need for Love

Both the bug lady and I needed more love. I needed to experience myself as more loving amid my button being pushed, and she needed to feel that she wouldn't be attacked either. We all need love, but sometimes we hide that need underneath layers of our accumulated pain and defenses. It happens at all ages. Since I chose to be defenseless with the bug lady, my chances of seeing the beauty in our encounter changed significantly, and I felt I was led by a power much greater than my own because my mind alone could not have anticipated the totality of our encounter when it initially saw negativity.

Through my prayer for guidance, I was led to abandon the

idea that insects were the problem and instead focus on my intuitive lead, creating a more positive interaction. By following that guidance, everything improved, including the insect issue. The insect issue wasn't what was asking for my attention; what was asking for my attention was improving the nature of our interaction.

Giving Away Our Power

Years prior, I might have reacted in defense to her rather than choose to maintain my defenselessness, but reacting to her defense with my defenses would have bred fear and ultimately changed nothing. I knew that when I have reacted in my past, no matter how strong or loud I was, I was only proving that I was powerless to the influence of another person. Makes us wonder what true power is, doesn't it? In my past choices to be defensive, I had cut myself off from my guidance and gave away my power to someone or something else. (On that note, when people purposely or unconsciously provoke us into defensiveness, they are merely testing how much control they can exert over us.) On the day of the bug lady, however, I was prepared. I had asked for God's help and was guided to a solution that I couldn't have known would happen because my mind wouldn't have gone there willingly.

Building Trust

I often wonder how different our interactions would become if we asked for God's help and then allowed our intuition to guide the way around our shortcomings gently. It is up to each of us to create our own rules based on our own guidance for each circumstance and follow the intuitive lead that feels right to each of us. In this way, we can develop more trust within ourselves. I believe that our chances for success with anything will increase as we allow ourselves to show up in the way that we are being guided to show up instead of how we might be expected to show up.

Expecting Fear

The bug lady is one example of an entire world of people who expect us to show up like they do—in fear. We don't have to give that fear back. The answer to someone's fear is not adding more of our fear to the situation. The answer is for us to shine. It is then that we make that age-old ultimate decision: love or fear? The bug lady's initial abrasiveness was nothing more than fear, as all negativity is nothing more than fear. It was more than likely her defense mechanism which came from countless negative interactions, that had transformed the shining of her bold light into a dim reflection over the wear and tear of time.

Inviting Love

"Do you see how good I am?" That was one of the first things she said after she began opening up. What the bug lady was truly asking me in jest was, "Can you give me permission to be myself right now? I've been beaten up over the years, and I'd love to feel like I can just be me and do what I love." When I recognized and acknowledged her, I genuinely fanned her flame. After that, she was chattering my ear off about how it used to be in the bug business, giving me all these extra tips and spraying extra places in my house for me.

Perhaps she was used to standing between a problem and the people who had a (bug) problem, who probably felt negative about their problem. She was used to absorbing a lot of their misplaced aggression. I wonder how many folks stopped long enough to acknowledge a job well done? I wrote down the bug lady's suggestions as well, which was even further acknowledgment, and when she noticed that, she kept on pouring out her wisdom.

Things aren't always as they seem. This old saying is true for prejudging appearances, but it is especially true regarding why situations happen as they do and what we can choose to learn from them if we ask for God's help in learning. In any circumstance where we doubt, we must *assume* that we are in the right place at the right time, even if we believe we perceive good or bad. The more we can accept where we are and what is going on around us, the quicker its true purpose will be revealed.

Spiritual Intimacy

Relating With Ourselves

Intimacy is the natural feelings-based relationship that we have with ourselves. In short, intimacy could be defined as how comfortable we feel in our skin and others. Whereas identity helps us define who we are to the outside world, intimacy helps us identify how we feel about our inside world. Our choice to allow our feelings to be felt is what cultivates spiritual intimacy. Within intimacy lies endless discovery.

Opening and Closing the Door

As we practice getting to know ourselves at the feelings level, we find that we have strengths, weaknesses, love, fear, pain, illusion and truth about who we are. When we open the door to how we feel, we encounter feelings that seem to be from all over the spectrum. Some are easy to face, and others are more difficult to face. Some feelings are painful; others may be pleasurable.

We tend to suppress feelings because of the discomfort that lies in allowing them to be felt. We don't always understand the benefit of feeling something, so we decide that it is better or even healthier to bury our feelings. Since the world does not value the expression of our feelings, we are taught not to make their expression a priority. We have taught ourselves to turn off how we feel so that we can manage our lives from a more comfortable standpoint from our mind's point of view. Since we've deemed that those feelings don't always serve our mind's agenda, we find that it is far easier to turn them off than to sort through them.

Compensating for Intimacy

Whether through instant trauma or slow wear and tear over time, our untrained minds inch ever more closely to shut the door to our feelings and self-intimacy—unless we declare to maintain an open door! After we become complacent, we begin insulating ourselves with security countermeasures. Whatever internal insecurity we have within us that we feel we cannot surmount, we attempt to create external security to compensate for it. Vehicles, homes, toys, money, even relationships can substitute for the feelings of safety that we feel we cannot provide to ourselves.

Objects as Insulation

Neutral objects such as homes and vehicles by themselves have no meaning. However, the meaning that we give to them reveals how we use them. That is, to expand or contract our sense of security. The more we fear intimacy and emotions, the more likely we will be to insulate ourselves with external forms of security countermeasures to prevent us from feeling what we do not want to feel.

Of course, it's not wrong to own material possessions. Materials can be used to open hearts and bring people together. But when we use these neutral objects to create separation and distraction from having to face ourselves emotionally, we do the disservice of inhibiting our self-intimacy and emotional development. Anything we own and any action we take will always be a choice between love and connection or fear and isolation, however small.

Isolation as Insulation

Sometimes we isolate ourselves using other people as insulation. Insulation from what, you ask? From facing how we feel inside. We decide who we allow into our circle of concern (insulation). Then once we are comfortable enough with our support system, we risk closing our hearts to outsiders (isolation). Isolation isn't only individualized; it can be highly socialized.

A subtle but potentially dangerous isolation tactic is gossip. It is risky to indulge in gossip because the ego tricks us into believing that judgment equals concern. Gossip is, ultimately, a need to seek out validation through comparison with other people. Feeling better through comparison creates insulation, which garners a false sense of security. Using a false sense of security to feel better creates isolation and separation.

Physical freedom doesn't necessarily equal spiritual freedom. Depending on our definitions, freedom could merely be an elaborate display of security mechanisms that ironically jail our inner freedom. To illustrate how much freedom we are ready to receive, remove the security mechanisms (insulation). The amount of spiritual growth and true security within oneself will soon become evident.

On the other hand, we can use our circle of concern as a springboard for keeping our hearts open! Even if we are afraid, we still don't want to live insulated, isolated lives. A family or group of loved ones focused on love and acceptance can lift each other out of gossip, judgment and insecurity into increased openness and acceptance of others. Again, we are choosing love or fear at any given moment.

Masters of Intimacy

Revered spiritual masters such as Mahatma Gandhi, who surrendered material possessions and isolation tactics, did not do so out of whim. It was not a mere spiritual belief that masters blindly followed. In the intimacy that these masters had nourished within themselves, they created a place of inner safety. They relied upon their relationship with God to provide sustenance, and God *did* provide. This meant that they had listened inwardly to their feelings, allowing for the acceptance and release of many wounds and fears. The resounding result within is feeling good, guided and supported. As we face love and heal our pains, our need to create external security recedes next to the resounding note that safety has been found within us. It is then that security slowly becomes solely derived from feeling peace. With no resistance, well-being abounds. When peace within is felt and maintained, external possessions and feelings of isolation or exclusivity become unnecessary.

We do not need to expend so much energy rearranging our external life to feel peace, but we can see a dramatic change when we allow our feelings to be felt instead of ignored. External actions are reflections of what is happening inside us. Ignoring our inner world leads to ignoring the outer world. Embracing our inner world leads to embracing the outer world. In our purging of the old feelings that bind us to the past, we become pure vessels to allow in all of the good things God wants to give us.

Self-Honesty Creates Intimacy

One way to enhance our self-intimacy is by being honest with ourselves about how we feel. Unfortunately, billions of us tell ourselves one thing when we are feeling something else. Playing politics with our feelings and struggling to rectify our inner opposing beliefs is what tears us apart inside. It creates misalignment and fragmentation within us. Our head goes one way, and our spirit goes another. This prevents us from feeling love for ourselves because we inundate ourselves with agenda followed by stress.

No matter how busy a schedule we have, it is possible to lead a peaceful life. But we need to make it a priority. The most challenging thing for us to face is keeping ourselves busy to avoid addressing how we feel. We self-medicate with drugs, alcohol, sex; you name it. We've done practically everything to try to change how we feel without allowing ourselves to feel what is there for us to feel.

We are starved for self-intimacy. We are desperate to know and feel ourselves, and at the same time, we are afraid to love ourselves. This ironic relationship shows us that we misunderstand transformation and that we have inner work to do. Our expansion is never-ending, and there will always be the next step to take. Recognition of our problem is half the battle, but awareness alone doesn't always resolve a problem. Many times, doing the inner emotional work is the needed other half.

To make positive changes, dare to ask those tough questions

like, "How do I really feel about this?" and, "Wouldn't I feel better if I expressed it to someone?" Posing a tough question can save us a lifetime of hardship because we were brave enough to be honest with ourselves when we needed it the most. Real spiritual growth isn't romantic and idealistic; it takes courage to face ourselves emotionally and experience true transformation and forgiveness. If we are doing the same spiritual practices yet we have the same personal challenges for years on end, it will take some self-honesty to admit that what we are doing is not providing us with significant transformation, development and growth.

Intimacy Creates True Security

Throughout our lives, we will always have a relationship with ourselves. Choosing to focus and manage how we feel about ourselves will yield gains far beyond any feeble attempts to maintain illusions of security. In this way, intimacy is a gateway into true security in our feelings, fortifying our actions, lives, and relationships with blessings and alignment with God.

Under every attempt we make to broach the outer world, we are looking for love. Everything we do is an attempt for us to feel better inside. Every action we take is to know feelings of safety and security, peace, love and joy. Yet, the quality of our actions yields questionable levels of success.

Life is designed to serve us, and it serves us best as we make self-honesty a high priority. The more we can align with treating ourselves with love and kindness through cultivating spiritual intimacy, the less we will seek it out in other things and people.

Prayer

Our Salvation Declaration

We are in the most powerful position ever because we are in a state of being where we are doing something good for us that is in direct opposition with everything our ego believes to be possible right now. The ego believes it can't be helped or feel better, so its domination reinforces that false reality. But we are choosing, nonetheless, to read inspiring things and to exercise our power. We have no clue what the result will be, and we don't know how we will feel when we're done. The only thing we know for certain is that we want to feel better. Because we don't have any answers, we have nullified ourselves into this state of being.

In making this choice, we are taking advantage of the perfect opportunity to do something positive for ourselves. We are choosing it, especially when we feel like there are no other options. This is the perfect time to pull out the weed at its root. This reinforces our inherent core power of strength to be in that state of darkness and choose light. One drop of light will illuminate an entire ocean of darkness. We keep choosing light until it grows stronger and stronger. It is of great benefit to be in this state of darkness because we are in full touch with how we do not want to feel, and our incentive for getting out of this state of being is strong.

The incentive had not been strong until now because the ego has cornered off every other option for expansion.

Therefore, it is from this place of pain, disillusionment and suffering that we begin, which is our most powerful place to choose from. To choose amidst the deepest pain and confusion and horror of feeling bad comes the greatest power of the I AM. This is trust. This is real. This is how we choose to be, and it is the foothold of all choices to rise upward. This realization of power at our Source, while present in our deepest darkness, is when we recognize once again that we are more powerful than any amount of darkness we feel and that we are not the darkness.

We begin to choose light gently. We feel a sense of power from this light. We feel a small shift upward. We no longer feel as bad as we felt before, so we decide to choose again in the upward direction. We continue to marvel at the power we just displayed where we previously made a choice that seemed to be from within absolute darkness, and we realize that even in our misery and pain, we rediscovered our power to choose. Our emotions begin following this new choice, and we reinforce more and more as we rise up that we are experiencing ourselves in our greatest glory. We are remembering ourselves while in our darkest hour. We are remembering our power to choose. This is the greatest display of divine power that we could hope to know of ourselves. This is our divinity, and it is more powerful than anything else we know about us. If we remember, from when we were in seeming complete darkness, we were still present with our true self, in all of our glory and power. We knew, deep down underneath, that the real I AM was there somewhere within us and that we just had to accept that we were in that darkness long enough to remember and rediscover the real power that we are.

Our minds begin to change dramatically at this point. By our acceptance, we begin to realize how helpful our pain has been to us and how much our struggle has meant to us. We remember this choice that we made while feeling at our worst that we had the ultimate opportunity to empower ourselves to be at our best.

The best that we could be for ourselves was choosing to remember who we were when we had forgotten—the Almighty I Am. When we felt bad enough, when we felt no incentive to try to change, when our world told us that there was no way we could make that change, when everything in our feelings told us that change was impossible, we still chose to remember the I Am.

We have rediscovered the light of God within us.

When we feel the absolute darkness within, we can intimately experience how infinitely bright our light truly is, and no matter how dark it gets, the light of God within us never ever burns out.

The Right Kind of Prayer

I've observed how some things that I've prayed for in the past have quickly manifested, while others, not so quickly. I noticed how when I began praying for the right things, I was given them. So what is praying for the right things?

Would it be practical for me to pray for a new car to manifest out of thin air when my desire is transportation to the next block? Wouldn't it make more sense for me to pray for transportation or even walk?

Here's another example: Let's say I believe I need a new job because things aren't going well at my current job. So I pray and pray for a new job, yet a new job doesn't show up when I prayed for it to show up. Instead of praying for a new job when I feel insecure, why don't I pray for *faith* instead?

Praying for the types of things that God can give us *now*, like virtues, is always easier for us to receive than praying for some future thing we have little control over.

Praying for the future

Although it's great to focus on the result when we pray, we must be careful not to project our results into a future time. This matters because the creative power that we have as humans lies in the present. Since our creative power is the power that we have *now*, our constant projection of ourselves into the future will not only make us feel less vibrant and present but it will also perfectly manifest that way. In other words, we perfectly create our present moment as the experience of having something later.

This means that every moment we expend trying to control some future moment will create the reality in the present moment of us repetitively experiencing wanting to receive such and such in a future moment. For example, "I know I'll get married in the future" might become an unfortunate mantra that exists well into our 80's if we don't practice praying for it in the present.

Receive it Now

If we want to receive it now, then we must *receive it now*. Pray to receive healing *now*. Pray to receive abundance *now*. As we ask for it, we must allow the feeling of it to arrive in our bodies. Don't struggle for it; just feel it. The goal is feeling it and enjoying it; experiencing it. This is not a mental exercise that you can succeed or fail at. Setting intentions repeatedly is not an effective course of action to receive because it's based on mistrust and lack. That would be like starting to build a sandcastle but destroying it and starting over before making any progress because we're afraid it might rain. Instead, let's make one intention. Then, let's spend all the rest of our time and energy *feeling* the reality of ourselves having what we asked for and receiving it.

The same goes for prayer. Let's not pray for something that God cannot easily provide us with now. We *can* pray for anything, but what will be granted to us quickly and efficiently by God, our Angels, and our Higher Selves will always be what serves our highest good, that which is in most alignment with us and that which we are allowing ourselves to receive.

Universally Supported

I sometimes get this vision of some of my angels sitting together playing poker. Some are smoking cigars with visors on, raising antes, sitting in wooden chairs with their wings draped over the backs of them, and of course, always listening. They always wait vigilantly with full attention, tuned into our requests, waiting to support us, waiting for us to pray with the right requests. They sit and relax because many of our requests are based on lack and victimhood. There's not much they can do to help us in those cases besides nudging us to ask the right questions and move in the right directions.

When we *ask the right questions, when we align* with our inner truth and Universal Law, those angels jump out of their chairs. Alarms sound, poker chips fly everywhere, chairs are knocked over in haste, cigar smokers choke and cough, and all of the aces of spades up their sleeves are left behind as the angels' priorities suddenly change. The poker room is empty. Instantly, they've rushed down to support our choices, prayers and requests in all ways possible.

Effective Prayer

As our consciousness growth continues, our prayers naturally become more effective. Some of the best prayers request that our blessings go toward the highest good possible for all involved. This is a spiritual prayer because it supports the best good instead of what we think is best. These additional blessings could help to make something good happen, prevent something unnecessary from happening, add a little bit more of what is needed somewhere, and so forth. A prayer asking 'to be guided in prayer,' for example, or 'to be of service to God and others' is a prayer that will always be supported. A masterful prayer requires incredible trust, acceptance of what is, and belief that what is happening is divine and set up for our perfect growth. Let's keep in mind that perfect growth isn't the absence of challenges but the recognition that they have been placed in our lives perfectly to be embraced and accepted.

Whenever we are in alignment with Universal Law, in alignment with ourselves, asking out of compassion and trust instead of ego or lack, we will generally feel (or even see) immediate results. So, for example, instead of praying for a new job, let's pray for *faith* in our ability to recognize that our request has been heard—and then receive it. Instead of praying that our obnoxious neighbor moves away, let's pray for *tolerance*—and then receive it. Instead of praying that we don't have to get up on stage and speak in front of others, let's pray for *courage* that we get through it okay—and then receive it.

The spiritual confidence that arrives with being courageous is the kind of self-actualization that cannot be unlearned. It's a testimony of self-recognition. This is not recognition of our mind's view of our human self but recognition of our spiritual essence, our power as Source consciousness and our awareness of God within us. Such faithful living is naturally

119

rewarded with fewer fears, more joyous presence, confidence, compassion, generosity and time to spare for others. Through our prayer, what once was a frantic mental effort to keep track of all aspects of our lives, comes the simple focus of one aspect in our lives—spiritual surrender.

Life happens with perfection, and we practice mastership when we allow it to serve us. It can seem burdensome at times, but we can learn to flow with life gracefully. When we have total trust and spiritual surrender, we eagerly anticipate each moment as an opportunity to recognize God in any situation. And unto each person's belief, it shall be done.

Surrender

Spiritual Surrender

Giving up?

We may think that surrender and giving up mean the same thing, but they are quite different when we consider these two terms from a spiritual perspective. Giving up is just what it sounds like—giving up or quitting. However, surrender is letting go and *accepting* what is happening in our lives right now.

Going with the Flow

Spiritual surrender is a doorway into an entirely different type of living. Surrender means gracefully accepting and going with the flow of our lives. Some may think that surrendering means that we must sacrifice or accept that we can't have what we want. This is entirely untrue. We can still choose what we want to have in our lives. However, the difference with surrender is that after we've made our desired choice, we allow it to arrive to us in faith at exactly the right time, place, essence, and fashion that serve our highest and greatest good. Essentially, we trust that life will work out for us.

Trusting Life

Surrender is not a concept that our ego favors because it

requires relinquishing ego. At first, we begin surrendering only a few of our choices to the Universe. After some practice and developed trust, we may decide to surrender some bigger things, like the directions of our careers and our relationships. When we become spiritually attuned to surrendering, we allow it to become our natural state of being, guiding all aspects of our lives. This means that we walk in a state of surrender every moment we live, trusting that everything that occurs—from the mundane to the extraordinary—is in divine right order.

Is it possible to accept that life will naturally and gently move us forward without our pushing and struggling? Of course, the ego would not have us believe this. Still, letting go more often (instead of attempting to control every aspect of our lives) will promote deeper acceptance of ourselves, our friends and families, and our life situations.

Creating Presence

We worry so much, don't we? Under the surface of any given day, there are countless things on our minds, most of which never arrive at the surface of our consciousness but rather arrive as underlying feelings of angst or mild emotional discomforts. We may not always know what it is, but we can feel it when it's there.

When we focus on this moment, without worrying about the next thing that may happen, we are creating presence, feeling at ease and peaceful. When we choose to remain at ease despite negative thoughts that attempt to lead us out of feeling at ease, we are consciously surrendering. Surrender and presence are closely related. Surrendering creates presence, and presence leads us to want to surrender more.

Our conscious focus on what is right in front of us is the best practice for our growth. This is especially helpful if we are easily led away from the present moment and into fear. It may not be glamorous, but there's always a reason for the condition of the present moment. As we practice feeling at ease with the present moment, our lives flow naturally. Unfortunately, the ego leads us to believe that focusing on the past or future is better than the present. The ego wants to bring us out of surrender and back into worry.

Placing ourselves where we are not—whether projecting into the future and past or creating cosmetic substitutions for ourselves—almost always leads us to disillusion and dissatisfaction. Our projection of ourselves into some other place or something other than what we naturally are causes misalignment.

Misalignment

We are no strangers to the types of neuroses of the mind and ailments of the body that can develop when we subject ourselves to any misalignment for extended periods. The process is always the same—energetic misalignment first, manifested misalignment second. Whether mild or severe, these misalignments eventually have wear and tear on our feelings. For example, when I have focused on the past or future for too long, I have felt somewhat desensitized or empty in my feelings. Things that used to feel full and fresh to me had begun to fade. This is because our power flows from the present. When we put too much attention into the past and future, it causes us to lose our sense of feeling at ease.

Guidance is Built-In

Our spirit lets us know when we are out of alignment with our feelings. It's built-in—we can't screw this up. When we're out of alignment, we don't feel good. When we are in alignment, we do feel good. Even when we don't have the answers, our feelings still guide us correctly and appropriately. A deep, built-in technology in us (God) always knows the appropriate direction to lead us, but we must surrender to access this technology fully. We must give up our controls fully to be led by a good that we cannot comprehend but is good for us.

There is infinite intelligence in our feelings, intelligence that transcends the boundaries of time and space. This intelligence will always be superior to the mind in functionality, efficiency and effectiveness. Feelings are products of the soul and spirit; emotions are products of the mind. Feelings are based on our inherent, deep inner truth, whereas emotions are disturbances, reactions from the mind. Silencing the mind can assist us in reaching our feelings which sometimes reside beneath the surface of our consciousness, depending on our alignment. Surrender, of course, is the first step in silencing the mind.

Surrender is an easy concept to understand but can be difficult to live. Studying and living surrender brings to awareness what we are dealing with—trusting versus controlling, believing versus manipulating, creating faith versus creating problems.

Creating Problems

As we observe the mind, we can see that it naturally seems to help us create problems. Without re-training the mind, we may spend the rest of our lives trying to overcome the problems that the mind has created. The mind can lead us into an endless cycle of chasing our tails without ever catching them. Surrender ends the tail-chasing cycle.

Surrendering will transcend the programming of the mind by helping us to remember our agreement with God. This is a process that occurs outside of the mind. I understand how elusive this must seem because what occurs beyond the mind is a process that we do not manage. It can be challenging to give up that control, give up those problems, and hand them over to God.

Creating Solutions

We can't expect to create a solution at the level of the mind when the mind created the problem. No real solutions exist at the level of the mind alone. Our surrendering, our going higher, and our accessing higher consciousness create a solution. This will be truthful for any problem's solution. To have a real solution, we must come from an awareness that is higher than the problem. If we want real change, we must access a bigger part of us than the mind alone. Although we do not understand the process of surrender, we can know its experience because it makes us feel at ease.

It Can Work for You

Surrender is for everyone. The ability that surrender puts us into touch with is built into all of us, and our expanding consciousness is the result—awareness. Awareness is the reason, the birthright of everyone: the young and the old, the unreligious and the religious, the uneducated and the educated. Surrender is a natural state for anyone to realize and maintain.

Living in Surrender

We are more than our minds, and we are not bound by our mind's seeming limitations and control over our consciousness. Through surrender, the nature of life itself begins to transform as our mind's dominance over our spirit recedes: feelings become clearer, truth becomes evident, regular guidance is accessible, miracles are ordinary. Deepening love and trust are all the natural results of surrender. In essence, surrender is the doorway to the awareness that we exist beyond the mind. Not only can we take regular trips beyond it, but we can also live beyond it with practice.

The Invitation

Be courageous. Surrender to what is. Accept the flow. Silence your mind. Raise your awareness. Evolve your consciousness. Fall more in love with yourself. Follow your joy and guidance, all in that order, if you wish. Observe the connection between the ego's inability to surrender control and the freedom available beyond its self-imposed limitation. Life wants to give you everything that you will allow yourself to receive. With the natural relinquishment of fear through surrender, trust becomes easy, and love naturally rushes in to meet you as you go higher with Source.

Spiritual Surrender: Part II

I Control My Life

I discover more each day about how surrender works in my life. With this awareness, I've noticed how much I attempt to control my life. When things have looked uncertain, I have tended to attempt to *control*. I've done it without even realizing it. When I have felt out of control, I have tried to control another person's behavior, which was my ego feeling the most threatened. Some of my ego's games are its insistence on doing things its way, its intellectual dominance games or its just plain whining.

As I've begun to realize how controlling things has *not* made my life work better, I've made correlations between *what* I was controlling, *how much* I was controlling it and *how controlling it created discord* as a result. These insidious control mechanisms were a shocking personal discovery. When I became disgusted enough with my controlling behaviors and their resulting stagnancy, I made a serious choice to surrender more often.

Control vs. Surrender

Control is the opposite of surrender, but to what degree are we aware of our controlling behaviors? The best thing I can recommend is to continually check-in, asking the Holy Spirit for guidance. Stating, "I surrender this" can be helpful to create the right kind of atmosphere for learning, leading to better results. When we let go of agendas, the need for attention, validation or approval, we can become aware of what it is we are attempting to dissolve.

I've observed how some aspects of my life have progressed while others have not. I came to discover that I had fear about those areas that were not developing. I had become so sick of the same patterns of recycling that I couldn't stand it any longer, but a solution never seemed to arrive. Development never seemed to blossom regarding certain things.

I chose to surrender because I felt I had no other choice. No other choice *led* me anywhere. I said, "God/Holy Spirit, I do not know the answer. I've surrendered before, but I didn't do it fully, or it didn't seem to last. I have no clue how to get through this. Please guide me through it. I want to mature and develop. I want to give up fear." The words I used were not important, but the desire and choice I had made were important.

Weeks later, as I remained committed to my vow to practice surrender and not fall back into old patterns, I began noticing myself making little discoveries. These blips on my radar began slowly coming through onto my screen of consciousness. The first instance was an entirely new thought on how to address something differently. Behaviors that I once considered normal I identified as defense mechanisms or blockages in my development.

I felt compelled to act on those opportunities before the newly-shining candle was doused. Before then, I would only have used my usual approaches to my problems. My ego would have tempted me to validate myself by doing things in my old, familiar ways, but I was determined to get out of that repetitive cycle. I knew what was not working for me because I had experienced enough of the same results. That's when I surrendered and began receiving new flickers of insight as if they were breadcrumbs leading me out of the darkness of my familiar thinking.

I Know Nothing

Ever hear of the phrase, "I know nothing?" It took me a while to learn what it means: empty yourself of what you *think* you know and allow the Holy Spirit/God to teach you. It means to empty yourself of *your* agenda and allow the Holy Spirit/God to teach you *His* agenda. This is what we are surrendering to—a higher power. This means learning how to listen to God's voice within us and learning how to recognize and deny the ego voice.

It seems to be our nature as humans to discover the valuable part of us, but then once we are happy with what we've discovered, we allow our ego to close our aperture once again slowly. What I mean by that is when we have found what we like about ourselves, we run the risk of allowing ego to overtake what we value and use it to create exclusion. Ego tells us that we now know. Then, we no longer have room to *receive* anything more because the ego has convinced us that *we think we now know.*

In a manner of speaking, "knowing more" *by ourselves alone* is what creates this separation from God.

Ever meet a "know-it-all?" I've taken on that role before, but I was unaware of the separation it caused between my Spirit and my physical self. When we "know it all," we close our aperture. We let in less light. We close our minds and our hearts to some degree. We've become complacent with what we know, and although valuable and validated by the world, being a know-it-all isolates us if we know it alone. Should the cost of becoming an expert be so steep?

The Surrendered Expert

A 'surrendered expert' allows his expertise to be in service of God instead of ego. We serve not because we are attached to the results of serving but because we are pointing the way back to love. In surrender, we may be experts, but we are more open to others' perspectives, not less open. Being an expert surrendered to God doesn't make us less accessible; it makes us more responsible.

When our experience melds with our gifts, and we trust our talents, we are surrendered. When we surrender, we allow our inner feelings effortlessly to blend and flow with our conscious mind without the mind interfering. In other words, before we give effort, we are naturally aligned. So, for example, 'beginner's luck' isn't lucky. It is a phrase given to the belief that applying mental strength is somehow more in alignment than being surrendered and unassuming.

Surrender allows us to feel peaceful instead of wanting; appreciative instead of jealous; peaceful instead of anxious; compassionate instead of suspicious; detached instead of expecting.

Surrendered Trust

When we choose to step back, we allow spirit to step forward and lead for us. I call it 'surrendered trust' because it can be easy to tell ourselves we are trusting, and yet we have layers of fear being felt directly underneath. Trust works when we allow it to serve us in transforming our emotions. Without transformation in our emotions, trust is merely a mental affirmation, and that isn't trust at all. In surrendered trust, peace begins to replace our discontent. We allow ourselves to be okay with not knowing the answers because we don't have to know. We let things be as they are without trying desperately to fix them. In surrendered trust, we don't cover up our discouragement and feelings of lack with affirmative platitudes as we *try* to manifest something. Manifesting occurs without effort when we surrender. In surrendered trust, we also give without expecting anything in return.

Surrendered Giving

'Surrendered giving' is giving because we are at peace, and we feel good by giving. Surrendered giving is sharing because we have something to share, not take. When we give something for psychological gratification or social (guilt) conditioning, we are taking, not giving. It is a game of the ego. I would even go as far as to say that if we are not giving peace by our giving, we're not giving anything at all.

Surrendered Expression

Surrender accesses our natural communications with our spirit. When we speak or express from the heart, for example, we are creating a 'surrendered expression.' We are in a *state* of surrender, and we flow from feeling good. Notice how easy the words come out when the flow is present and how good it feels to speak from the heart. Surrendered expressions can occur through talking, painting, dancing, basket weaving or Olympic Ice Curling. If our heart is in it, it's a surrendered expression.

Un-Surrendered Living: Spiritual Development vs. Ego Development

Ever have times when you could not stop thinking? I cannot emphasize enough the following sentence: we think to avoid experiencing and feeling. We put more importance on thinking than feeling. We tend to push forward our development in ways that we feel comfortable within our mind-made identity. Then, we have to figure out how to present that identity to others so that they know we're fulfilling that role we say that we are. We go to great lengths to put our identity out to the world, but is our heart and spirit in it too?

The Irony of Surrender: Manifesting Change

The ironic thing about surrender that many of us are still learning is that if we want to change, we need to surrender the change, not control what we want to change. Why does the change we want not occur? We are usually blocking the change, attached to the change, or the change isn't what our spirit desires (which often conflicts with what the ego wants). Here's the other half of it: when we surrender the need for controlling the change, the resistance we feel *leaves* us.

134

"I feel the resistance leaving me as I surrender. That's weird. I thought I *needed* that object/thing?" you say. The irony is not that we wanted change and didn't get it. The irony is that the place from which we do the wanting, the ego, is *not real.*

"Why can't I manifest?" underneath the truth-magnifying glass is translated as, "*I don't trust God or myself.*" When we do trust, we don't count the days on the calendar. Time has nothing to do with our salvation because we are at peace.

The good thing is that it's not the real us that doesn't trust; it's the ego. Isn't it interesting how the wanting for more reveals the truth within our illusions? We say we're not getting what we asked for, but we are indeed receiving it! *We are creating and receiving the opportunity to gain the awareness of why our life isn't working the way we think it should so that we can have what God wants for us.* We just need to recognize and trust Him and ourselves.

When we have truthfully surrendered, change will happen if we've asked for it. If it's not the change we expected, surrender will ensure our peace regardless. When we have truthfully surrendered, the change we tried to control *is no longer in our mind.* If we have surrendered, we have found peace. We have given our minds to God.

Real Solutions: Surrendering Our Minds

A solution of the mind arrives at the level of the mind. The mind may appear to dissolve a problem, but it merely prolongs the problem. The problem *is* the un-surrendered mind. When our minds believe we are creating a solution, we are merely negotiating internally about what we will accept or not accept. We take inventory of our value systems and fears, and we explore possibilities. Our unhappiness does not come from our life situations. It comes from trying to create a solution in the mind. Surrender is what gets us out of the mind and into the guidance of the Holy Spirit.

Salvation and solution do *not* exist at the level of the mind. We cannot think our way out of our problems. Thinking may help us step toward acceptance, but it doesn't create a solution. A real solution *heals* the mind and its errors in perception and returns it to God through surrendering to the Holy Spirit. A real solution creates peace. A surrendered mind is at peace, not compromised.

Daily Intentions

As often as I can remember, I make daily intentions to give up my control over everything, especially anything that gives me concern. If something is meant to happen, it will happen more quickly through the Holy Spirit working through me than through my unconscious fearful interference in controlling it. If action is required, it will be surrendered action, not fear-based action.

God, let me make no decisions by myself. I listen in silence for instructions. I focus all my attention on what is happening now. I experience my life with ease. I step back, and I allow You, Holy Spirit/Holy Father, to lead the way. I allow You to teach me love and compassion for myself and others.

Being: The State of Spiritual Surrender

Beyond Surrender

When I surrender, I can let go of my worry (at least temporarily). I know I have surrendered once I am feeling relieved or relaxed. But what about going beyond that? Am I just supposed to wobble back and forth between surrendering and not surrendering things for the rest of my life? Sure, I might get out of my mind for a while, but I usually find a way to get back into it because my worry always seems to return. Let's go beyond the act of surrender and go straight into the act of *being*.

What is Being?

Being is the state of surrender. It is feeling the connection that we have with our Source. Being is accepting this moment as it is without worrying about it. Essentially, being can't be understood. It can only be felt. If the mind uses thinking to communicate, then being uses feeling to communicate. It is challenging for many of us to get into being purposefully and regularly because we want to think more than we want to feel. Because even when we try to feel, we are usually trying to feel with the mind. Being is felt, not thought.

The Need for Being

When I put my mind ahead of being (or thinking ahead of feeling), I tend to forget being, and I let my mind run my life. When this occurs, I get out of touch with feeling myself from the inside. I put all of my consciousness into my mind. I have then become my thoughts. I have become my reactions. There is no me between what I think and how I act. My mind is why so many platitudes and affirmations exist, and yet it doesn't get the job done until I truly accept the meanings behind them.

On the other hand, when I put my being before my mind, I am putting my consciousness (awareness and attention) into my body and the now moment and not into the future and past. When I direct my attention and awareness into my body and feel the energy and the presence within myself, I am putting being first. I am not a 'human later' or 'human past'— I'm a human being.

How to Put Being First

Meditation is a great way to connect with being. Meditation is nothing more than breathing and feeling the body with our attention. It's so simple we may question whether we are doing it correctly. It is that simple, and it doesn't require the mind.

In meditation, it helps not to engage in any thinking but to allow thoughts to pass through and keep attention in the body and on our breathing. All we're doing here is noticing the body. We don't need to think, look for insights, channel or have any expectations about how we feel or what we accomplish. Being happens naturally as we relax. Any insights or healing will come forth as needed. Remember, this is a process that the mind does not manage, so it may feel odd at first not to use the mind. The goal for connecting with being through meditation is not necessary to achieve anything. It's just a space for feeling and breathing. It's that simple.

The Gateway to Being

Attention on the body is a great gateway into being because it anchors our consciousness in the present moment. As we focus attention on how we feel on the inside, we may notice some changes. Our thinking will (eventually) slow down. We may notice some physical or emotional pain arise because the mind was suppressing it. Our breathing will naturally deepen and open up. We may cry, laugh, feel good, bad or not feel much at all. We're just providing the space to allow whatever needs to happen in us to happen. All we need to do is focus our attention on the body and breathing.

We are increasing circulation, setting the stage for emotional and physical healing, allowing mental detoxification, enhancing our internal communications and connecting with our Source. Again, we're not searching for anything. This is just what naturally happens.

Consciousness Follows Focus

Wherever I put my attention is where my consciousness travels. If I am always thinking, I am putting all of my consciousness into the mind. I can also direct my consciousness into other places within me. As I direct it inward and just notice—just feel—I am connecting to deeper levels within me. When I create the regular time to connect with being, I establish the remembrance of the strong connection that is always inside me.

A Train with No Engine

When I use the mind as primary over being, I can be like a detached train boxcar with no engine or cargo, unaware of which track I am riding on. I accelerate or slow, not by choice, but by the grade of the track around me. When I am like a detached boxcar, I succumb to the ups and downs that occur around me. When I let my mind run rampant, I am practicing little awareness of my spiritual power because I fall victim to whatever the world is throwing at me. If the people around me are afraid, I am afraid. I've lost my power.

A Powerful Locomotive

When I choose to use the mind as secondary to being, the mind becomes a wonderful tool for my creative expressions. Being is the powerful engine that carries the mind forward into service. I become like a steadfast, powerful locomotive engine full of coal and cargo to be delivered. When I allow my being to carry me, I allow my mind to relax. I am carried forward by the Source that is within me through surrender. Source *is* the engine that carries me forward.

When I let go and allow the mind to relax, I don't force myself to keep answering what the world throws at me. As I calm down, the things happening outside of me seem to calm down too. I may still have things I need to do, but I choose to relax as I get them done instead of stressing out too much as I get them done. When I do anything while connected to being (the state of surrender), my efforts are imbued with a sense of alignment, grace and being carried and guided. It's just easier to flow through life when I'm not stuck in my mind.

Fear Equals Misalignment

Worry or fear creates misalignment. For example, I have tried helping others when I have been afraid of what others might think of me if I didn't help them. I've wanted to help, but I was unaware that part of my motivation came from fear. I was not helping anyone by fearing for them. Energetically, I was lowering my vibration to others' energy levels when I worried about helping them. Help is not about fearing for others; it's about creating alignment in others, and it cannot be done when I am out of alignment. The most helpful person in any crisis is the one who stays the calmest, aligned and connected to being.

If I want to help someone, it is wise to align myself in being where a person desires to go but not aligning with their misalignment. My alignment is most easily accomplished as I choose to be relaxed. That way, they can follow me to my place of being relaxed. If I come from calm, then I am serving them. If I come from worry, I am not serving them. No matter how knowledgeable I may be at my craft, my misalignment only creates another problem for those I may attempt to help.

We Aren't Our Minds

When we are not connected to being, we believe that we are our minds. Getting still and relaxed isn't always easy, nor is it appealing for the mind, but once we arrive there, it does become easy. The mind is an amazing tool, but it isn't meant to run our lives. We know that is true because of how we feel while we are overrun by it. There are aspects to living that are hard for the mind to accept because it isn't meant to manage them. Life is hard when living from the mind alone. It's easier when we relax and flow with it.

Drama vs. Acceptance

There is a difference between perpetuating negative drama versus releasing and cleansing our emotions. Although they may look the same at first glance, the first is resistance, and the second is acceptance. When we complain about our challenges, we speak from our minds and give away our power to heal and accept. When we align with people who persuade us into their negative influence, we give away our power to exercise independence. When we want drama over peace, we stay in the mind.

We Are Source

We are Source consciousness rooted in being that can also think. We have much more Source consciousness available to us than we use. A whole universe lies in our ability to feel and to go beyond the mind. "I think, therefore I am" may prove that we exist, but it does not prove that the mind defines our existence. For centuries, thought has been the dominant definer of our existence. Still, we are discovering that our true reality as a 'Source consciousness being' points the way to

God within us in a way that the isolated thinking mind could never grasp.

Guidance from Our Being

Feelings are reference points to where we are standing as well as tools that guide us into being. "Bad" (or negative) feelings guide us just like positive feelings do. Yet, what we are feeling does not indicate anything definite about that particular thing. What feelings do indicate is our relationship to that thing. The difference is that negative feelings tell us what is not appropriate for us, and positive ones tell us what is appropriate for us. The key to following the guidance of our being is putting our attention towards those things that feel good and are in alignment.

Food For Thought

But what about the times when something that feels good is bad for us, like alcohol, drugs or excessive eating? These actions are taken to feel better and are based on the mind's need for relief. Emotional eating, for example, feels good, but it is the mind that is being appeased. This masquerades as what we are feeling, but the mind is the source of the emotion in actuality. The body doesn't crave excessive food; the mind does.

Using excessive food as an example, returning our attention inward will clarify the true relationship with ourselves—through stillness. Our choice to enhance our connection with being will enhance our connection to our body, mind and spirit. We will feel what our body needs more than what our mind wants, and this feels better.

143

Compulsive Thinking

Compulsive thinking has been one of the hardest habits for me to break. The mind is so powerful that it can continually disturb our inner connection, but it can never permanently disconnect it. It's good to look for relief, but we tend not to want to stop thinking. I know that I'll slow down, but I resist stopping altogether. In my mind's assessment, there is no payoff in silence, so it wants to avoid it. We find another party or another external stimulation to keep our minds engaged and entertained.

Until We Are Ready

I'm not saying we need to force ourselves to meditate. Forcing anything before we are ready and before we feel called to act is not a good idea, even if it seems ideal. We all naturally and intuitively know how to create balance within ourselves. We intuitively know how to meditate, and we do it all the time. We choose our practices to connect with being naturally. We paint pictures, write, nap, talk, relax, drive. Yet, each of us has our threshold of resistance. We experience a point where we don't want a stronger connection to 'being,' or we don't know of a stronger connection because we haven't experienced one yet. However, a stronger connection is available, and it is limitless.

When we are ready, we choose in some way that we want something better for ourselves. By some intuitive process, we naturally know when it is time to abandon an old way of thinking or behaving that no longer serves us. When we choose this, we feel better. The more we need to make a healthy choice, the more courage it may take. The good thing is that we can make healthy choices regularly, and they can become easier to choose because our connection to our guidance strengthens.

By choosing to get into 'being' more often, we can access parts of ourselves waiting to be used. We are more likely to make a beeline to whatever it is we want for ourselves because we strengthen the connection within by putting being first.

I have days when I don't have any desire to put being first. I'd rather sit on my rump. Some days, I just want to do what my mind wants to do, and that is all. Sometimes, a big pepperoni pizza is the only cure for what I've got. And is that wrong? No, it's not. Any choice that feels right to me is just fine for me. This is also an example of putting being first because I choose the choice that helps me relax my mind.

Making Being a Priority

Making being a priority adds nothing but good to our lives. Taking the time to 'be' creates the alignment with all that we desire. There's an often-used expression "putting God first." When we put feeling and being first, we are putting God/Source/Holy Spirit first. When we connect with being, we allow ourselves to be guided by Source and doing enough of it trains our minds to bring that state of being into our daily activities. Then, miracles start happening. We start spontaneously showing up at the right time for people. We get that phone call we've been waiting for. Something we've been trying to sell finally sells.

Being is Willingness

Relaxing and becoming silent creates alignment in our lives because we are choosing to give our willingness to God by doing so. The compulsive mind will lead us to believe that we aren't being productive enough and urges us to do more, but the relief rarely comes, and when it does, it is short-lived and never frees us from repetitive cycles. While we may be doing more on the outside, we may be losing something on the inside—our connection to being.

"Compulsive doing" is another ploy of the mind to prevent us from experiencing being. To the mass mind, sanity is a miracle, but to the Source within us, sanity is accessible to us at any time by our willingness to connect with being.

Our Personal Game

All life's troubles boil down to a game that I play with myself until I am ready to release the game. Even when I hate the game, I am still choosing it. It is me versus me. Yet, when I am willing to play it God's way, I feel good. When I am willing to go within, connect to being, let myself relax, not think for a while, breathe, and put my attention on my inner body, I let that peaceful practice carry me through all of my days. Yes, I do trust the Source in me to carry me through and into being. All things are done through the Source in me when I am willing to align with it. Anything that relaxes me or enlivens me, or makes me passionate will align me with my Source. I can do it all day long. Feel, relax, align. Just being me is enough.

Beyond the Ego-Mind

You Are the Gatekeeper

You Have the Power

Did you know that you are the gatekeeper of your thoughts? You have the power to choose which thoughts you will entertain. You have the power to have a healthy self-image and believe good things about yourself. Thoughts that do not feel good to you are not worthy of your attention. There is no need to entertain those thoughts. Entertain 'good feeling' thoughts. There is nothing more important in your life than that you feel *good*.

Choose New Thoughts

You do not have to struggle to move beyond a challenge. You need not overcome or defeat any bad or dark thoughts. Attempting to defeat dark thoughts will give them power. You can move through challenges gracefully and with acceptance of your present situation. You don't need to create conflict, additional hardship or fear. Choose new thoughts. Choose new thoughts *as soon as you notice* the thoughts that don't feel good to you and *feel* the new good feeling thoughts. Good feeling thoughts will attract more of the same.

Struggle is a Choice

Life may occasionally present challenging scenarios, but struggle must be *chosen*, and fears must be *remembered* as a substitution for your real self, whether done unconsciously or consciously. The degree of resistance or internal struggle that we feel is determined unconsciously and involuntarily before we are presented with the situation. Many so-called struggles and even triumphs are delusional battles between the ego and the person who claims it, played out in an externalized scenario.

Getting Ego's Approval

The mental-emotional resistance pattern that tempts us to react instead of accept is called the ego-mind. It's the built-in survival mechanism we all have which is designed to protect us. The ego-mind resists us when it feels its sense of survival is threatened. This resistance is the ego's way of saying, "You must get my approval before I allow you to go any further." It then persuades us to believe that we must appease its programming for us to "triumph," which is ego's substitution for our union with God. Ego likes to convince us to overcome instead of detach and withdraw its power.

Ego Blesses Struggle

The ego blesses our struggle because it knows that we are further away from discovering its control over us when we do. For example, the ego-mind's influence is evident when we make a situation into a problem. It doesn't want us to accept something as it is. Ego's goal is for us to appease it, to put energy back into it and, if possible, to get us excited about the problems it offers us. If we identify with it and *enjoy* the problem, issue, or situation (i.e., complain, gossip, backbite), ego wins again. Ego's win is stronger if we enjoy the drama because the ego will remain in disguise if we are unaware that we are happily peddling its agenda. We enjoy the marionette show but are unaware that something is holding the strings behind the scenes. Ego's survival is then not threatened but strengthened.

Digging Deeper into Problems

We don't want to be deceived by ego's persuasion that by *struggling* or *overcoming,* we are accomplishing some grand mission or something special in accordance with our goals. We may still accomplish our goals. We may still work hard to achieve them and realize a job well done, but our choice to struggle, our choice to dig deeper into the problems to try to figure them out, is what *increases* ego's control over us. Doing so robs us of our spiritual freedom and cuts us off from the flow of well-being. The goal of spiritual growth is to dis-identify and *not* to struggle. The goal is to let go, step back, surrender, and allow the flow of life to move through us with ease.

Growing Beyond Struggle

No matter how good we get at living life, we will always encounter challenges. It's healthy to have challenges because they help us refine what we want. The key is to allow those challenges to serve us instead of limit us. If we are allowing life to *serve* us, it's a challenge. If we are allowing life to *limit* us, it's a struggle. If we let our lives be defined by our struggles, then we allow our lives to be run by our egos. The goal isn't to triumph over all of the struggles; the goal is to grow beyond the need for the struggles.

We constantly negotiate with ego's agenda when we allow it to determine our limitations. The extent to which ego's agenda controls us equals the degree to which we choose to identify with it. The more of an identification we hold, the more tightly ego holds us in its grasp. For example, through ego, the worse our career is going, the worse we are feeling about ourselves.

How We Lose the Present Moment

Did you know that ego's goal for us is to *lose the present moment*? Ego wants us to bring our past pain with us to create pain in our future. In this way, our present is covered up with the past and future. Ego ensures that whatever we accomplish will be through struggle. Our intentions may be strong, but our conscious presence needs to be strong also. If we allow ego to cover up the present moment, we prevent ourselves from exercising our spiritual power. If the ego-mind accomplishes this, it controls us.

With enough time passing under ego's influence, it can subtly erode more of our powerful presence into unconsciousness and keep us living in the past and future without being rooted in the vitality of the present. This is one interpretation of what it means to be unconscious. We may have external power (i.e., financial, political, physical), but being unconscious is 'unrealized internal power' (i.e., spiritual). Ego's control over us makes our reactions automatic and predictable.

Power in the Present

The only true power we have is in the present moment. By exercising our divine right as the gatekeeper of our experience, we determine how conscious or unconscious our experience will be. Will we allow the ego-mind to control us by keeping us lost in past pains or future worries? Will we react or defend? Will we hide behind platitudes and other conditioned, automatic reactions? It's our choice. As we find ways to be present and express our joy and true nature, as we lose the agenda and reclaim our power, we become the gatekeepers. The more we practice being here and now and are not dominated by our struggles, the less likely ego will trick us into moving into the past and future. Thus, we lose our All-Powerful Presence and Infallible Spiritual Power as Source Beings.

Love and Accept Ego

The ego is a part of us, an outdated mechanism struggling to keep up as we evolve. We want to observe the ego's programming in us when it comes up but not engage it. Instead, we want to love and accept ego as a part of us. Understanding it helps us become aware of its influence and accept it for what it is—a part of us that needs love. With acceptance, its influence dissolves.

Instead of negotiating with ego via struggling to overcome, consider becoming the gatekeeper. Before our ego-mind convinces us that we must work through the resistance it

153

wants us to face, that some old issue is slowing us down or has some influence over our future before ego convinces us that we are limited, afraid, incapable, shy or unable to achieve something, close that gate, gatekeeper! Before the ego-mind persuades us to react or defend or manipulate or convince us that a justifiable action is helping us to "get ahead"—stop.

Choose new thoughts. Choose positive thoughts. Notice how the positive thoughts feel to you. You are the gatekeeper of your experience, and you can experience as much joy or as much struggle as you wish. You decide whether ego stays inside the gate. Be the one who finds the gift in every moment through graceful acceptance and non-struggle. Be the gatekeeper of your thoughts, and watch a new world reveal itself to you. You are powerful!

Losing Identity, Gaining "I Am"

Growing Spiritually

We tend to think of spiritual growth as something we work on or learn. Some of us consider it a matter of how we feel our way through life, maintaining a steady balance of living truthfully. We could say that each interpretation is correct. As we seek, we find.

In our earliest steps during our quest for spiritual growth, we first look for validation of what we are experiencing on many levels. We ask others for permission that it is acceptable to feel the way we are feeling. In time, we begin to develop self-trust and listen to our inner voice. We learn to go within for truth about who we are and connect with Source.

As we search for truth, we may occasionally encounter things that don't feel all that good to us. We then tend to revert to something that feels familiar instead of stepping into the unknown. Although there is nothing wrong with falling back into a familiar routine, doing so does have its cons. What causes us to fall back into complacency is the mind. We use this tool to interpret and analyze our feelings, and while this is completely natural, it can cause considerable limitations in our spiritual growth. Spiritual growth is ultimately about the healing of the mind, so we need to remember that working on anything spiritual can be helpful as long as our efforts help us to release and step forward versus identify and remain mental.

Losing Identity

A common misperception about spiritual growth is that we become more than we once were or build upon who we are. It is only natural to feel that we would grow spiritually in the way that we have lived our physical lives. We tend to measure our success in the physical realm by what we've gained. Spiritual growth, however, is not a subject-object dichotomy, nor is it a process by which we build more onto our identity. Spiritual growth, rather, is the relinquishment of ego-identification. Spiritual growth is not a process by which we become more; it is a process by which we strip away who we are not. It is the process by which we lose what is not real in us and recognize what *is* real in us.

The uncovering of our perceived identity is a natural process of change that takes place in our consciousness. We eventually shed outdated mental ideas about ourselves, of what we believe ourselves to be and do. The nature of this change can cause confusion at times, multiplying our emotional responses and causing us to question our feelings and personal truths. As we naturally make our way through the confusion, however, we begin to understand that spiritual growth is not something meant to be learned so much as it is experienced as something that we recognize as we unlearn what is not true about ourselves.

We have taught ourselves untruths about who we are, and we live our lives with those untruths as our template for living until we spiritually awaken. As we wake up to the truth of who we are, we understand that there is nothing in us that is not perfect or not whole. We continually evolve our beliefs and perceptions about who we are as we naturally move into a clearer awareness and consciousness.

Through our learning, we remember how to recognize, which can be experienced as insight, revelation, a knowingness of truth. In learning, we are teaching ourselves something. In recognition, we perceive with clarity. Learning and recognizing work together to serve us. When we recognize truth, we no longer need to learn for the moment. Because we are recognizing (or remembering) our true nature rather than learning it, we come to understand that we can fully recognize our true selves at any moment.

Ego Identity

We have a general idea about how we grow spiritually. We know that we develop a mental identity to facilitate our learning of who we are. Identity is a helpful placeholder that we use throughout the chapters of our lives. So let's take a closer look at what identity is.

I've observed that how I feel about other people is almost always an indicator of how I feel about myself. Yes, I can sense and know that my feelings guide me and that the Law of Attraction is always governing how I interact with my world. Yet, my ego identity always has something in mind to maintain separation and the preservation of its existence within me.

We see ourselves in other people by how we feel about them. Our interactions with strangers can be a great indicator of how we relate with ourselves (especially when driving vehicles). I base this on the premise that "interacting with others equals interacting with ourselves" because when we are in full alignment with ourselves—when we are not suppressing our feelings; when our energies are balanced—we are in a state of grace. The natural state of the human being is one of love, acceptance and innocence. Children are an excellent example of that state.

Without recognizing the ego's presence, we can easily mistake ego for who we truly are. Ego is our perceived identity or our false identity. Our real identity is in God, the I Am. We spend so much of our time automatically sifting through our experiences and "working on our spirituality" that we forget what we are moving towards and what we are detaching from. This can only create confusion.

Essentially, we are growing into the awareness of oneness and union with God by learning how to relinquish our need for perception, thus detaching from ego's influence. When we recognize our false identity, we can free all energy and consciousness that the falseness had been suppressing within us and return to wholeness. We can call this process the Atonement (At-one-ment). We naturally seek out this unification with God, and we can recognize our union with God through any means we put our attention towards. We don't even need to call the lifelong realization of this process spiritual. It is spiritual by default. (See *A Course in Miracles* for more information on Atonement.)

Our ego identity wants us to appease it by acknowledging and embracing it and by valuing it. Ego wants us to resist unification ("At-one-ment"), which it perceives as a form of attack. It wants us to remain ignorant of its influence and confused about the I Am and the ego. The ego wants to control us, but it does not want us to know that we are being controlled by it. Any thoughts of attack that we have, for example, are prime symptoms of being influenced by it. What ego desperately does not want us to know is that our attack on others is an attack on ourselves.

Thought Projections

Once again, thought about others is merely thought about ourselves, a mental projection from our inner feelings. We believe that we're thinking about others, but we're not. Instead, we're thinking about how we feel about ourselves in relationship to others. The ego, however, persuades us to believe that a negative thought about others is something that they own, but this isn't true. A negative thought about others is, in fact, something that we own. Whatever we dislike in others, we dislike in ourselves. If the ego can convince us that the negativity we feel is someone else's problem, then the ego has won again in preventing us from healing the split in our minds. As we recognize that perceiving ourselves as different from others is a split in our minds, ego loses control over us. Without this recognition, however, we enable ego to dominate our minds and continue to confuse us, perpetuating our illusion of what we think is our identity and what we believe to be true of other people.

Clouded Answers

When we get lost in the ego-mind's influence, our search for answers becomes clouded because we must appease our beliefs, programming, associations, conditioning and any falsehoods that ego has persuaded us to believe, either via ourselves or the egos of others. The lies of the ego are endless, and its demise is in sight when it fails to prevent our arrival at an immutable truth. Ego fools us by reinforcing its identity as our own, and we mistake these short-lived, seemingly positive emotions for growth, gain, or even truth. Yet, we aren't always discovering a truth when we feel good. Sometimes our egos conceal the truth from us, masquerading illusion as something real. This is what perceived identity is— illusion.

Nevertheless, our consciousness evolution is perfect and will always take us in a perfect, natural direction. No matter how long we choose darkness, there is ultimately nowhere to go but God. Whether or not we work on ourselves consciously, we may still find ourselves looking for truth and stability within the unstable changes of life we can rely on—a truth beyond our loss of perceived identity. And, of course, it is human nature to feel darkness (i.e., instability, fear, uncertainty, doubt) when our truth is changing.

The Darkness

Many have called these painful times in consciousness rebirthing the "Dark Night of the Soul." It is a time in which our identity evolves at the soul level. We break through to expanded consciousness and, thereby, an expanded version of our self. The Dark Night of the Soul could be seen as the loss of mental identification with self. Mental identification is the filter through which spiritual knowledge is lost.

If we try to be something different from I Am, we may wonder why part of our identity appears absent. In such instances, we experience darkness or a detachment from God or I Am or a detachment from the most recent version of the truth about who we are. *A Course in Miracles* speaks of this as the resurrection and the crucifixion, which can occur as often or as rarely as we like. Some believe that the Dark Night of the Soul process is a one-time, lasting occurrence, whereas others maintain that it is a process that can occur multiple times in one life. For simplicity, we could define the dark night (or nights) as what we may experience as we arrive at the spiritual understanding or recognition that we are more than what we had previously perceived ourselves to be: a process of our consciousness evolving. The Dark Night of the Soul could also be described as the attachment to the pain of losing our identity.

Getting a New Grip on God

It is wise for us not to resist going through the Dark Night of the Soul because it is a part of our human experience. So many growth opportunities are lost due to our choices to push away or suppress what we would judge about ourselves instead of accept. Yet, it is also important for each of us to question for ourselves our processes of growth. It is up to us to decipher the difference between accepting the Dark Night versus allowing it to victimize us. If we allow it to victimize us, we can feel jailed for a long time without understanding what is happening.

It is natural to experience both pain and freedom while experiencing the Dark Night. Yet, although our spiritual connection is changing, it is important to remember that God never leaves us. We change in our orientation to Him.

It is often necessary to let go of our grip entirely to gain a new one. It may feel like we could fall, but our grip is sure as we grab on again.

If we have no expectations of what we think we should be, if we hold an open acceptance about our changing nature, if we leave our ideas of ourselves up to God to share with us, we would be less likely to encounter a backlash of experiencing who we are not. With the total acceptance of our experiences of ourselves, we resist nothing. We are constantly expanding and inviting in more of who we are, so when we don't choose to expand, we seem to choose the dark night by default. Embracing and allowing our change in identity gracefully and without attachment can ease the transition of our dark nights.

"Hey, I'm Human"

Of course, sometimes life just hurts! We integrate massive amounts of experience and balance tremendous energy around us. We don't always know how we are doing it, but we do. It's in our nature to evolve energy in us and around us. We experience the least pain and the most joy by practicing total acceptance of ourselves. Acceptance and non-attachment are priority number one.

When we integrate new energy, our ego can react, and we may find it defending itself against nothing—or anything or everything. Our ego-mind will occasionally search for what it can devise into a belief system, naturally probing for its promise of security, looking to gain a foothold once again within us. But, ultimately, it will disappear.

With the perceived identity falling away, the I Am beneath is revealed in our consciousness. This is the full recognition of God within coming to the forefront of our awareness. We experience ourselves as brand new in the I Am and without our previous filters, which have fallen away. We may feel a different type of connection, perhaps relating differently to ourselves than in the past. We naturally observe how we've been controlling so many aspects of our lives, and we feel comfortable practicing graceful surrender. We no longer resist the change but instead begin to flow with our new consciousness. We find that prior shifts caused upheaval within us, but subsequent ones seem to lift us into more alignment and clarity.

We begin to realize that we can now go within and create anything we need. The old schematic does not bind us. Even though the world still exists around us, we feel the birthing of the new world within us. We have a new and different type of access to our inward-dwelling divinity. We feel we have something to give. We no longer require protection because we are not in fear. We no longer need to wait for celestial alignments for optimal results nor deliberate until something or someone arrives to empower us to make positive choices. We trust our ability to choose.

Consciousness Is

The nature of consciousness is such that as we grow in awareness, we heal our minds. The most profound growth is unrecognizable at first and requires that we learn. Our internal change is condemned by our ego instead of acknowledged as a perfect process in motion. We have all gone through our share of struggles, yet our lives' surrender and expression work brilliantly for creating freedom and peace within us.

Our changing identity may have altered how we view our

spiritual growth, but what we are in our core being—in spirit—has not changed. We are learning how to allow ourselves to experience more of what lies beyond the mind. As we focus on avoiding mental engagement, such as remaining non-judgmental, being present in the now, we will continue to be in better union with God. We can live more freely with less mind by practicing non-attachment to what we do and who we've been and trade that in for God. We can feel this honesty as we look around at what people are expressing and how they express it, whether through writing or speaking or doing their favorite type of spiritual work. Surrendering the ego to God can be painful for the ego identity, but it leaves behind what is real and present, to begin with—the I Am.

The Law of Attraction

165

The Law of Contraction

Expansion or Contraction

The Law of Contraction is not a universal law. It is merely a phrase I created to describe what my life feels like when I am on the opposite side of the fence, so to speak, of the Law of Attraction. The Law of Attraction is always working no matter what, but depending on how we choose to use it, we are always either in a state of expansion or contraction. Expansion means that we are allowing ourselves to feel what we like and want. Contraction means that we are experiencing what we do not like or do not want. In this article, I will examine some of the themes that cause us to create contraction. Let's create some awareness by pulling out some weeds!

How We Block What We Want

How we block what we receive in our lives depends upon how much we resist (contract) versus allow (expand). We are in a natural state of allowing before we learn how to resist. So whatever we don't resist, we naturally allow. For example, we might allow great development in areas of personal growth while we resist the development of relationships with others. Or we might have great financial literacy yet be afraid to look for a job. If we think the Law of Attraction does not seem to be working for us somehow, it is likely because we don't want what we think we want, we block ourselves, we are mind-identified, or we feel lack.

We Don't Want It

Do you see anything in your closet that at one time you wanted but do not want anymore? Sometimes we think we want things, but we don't. When we obtain things through want and get bored with them quickly, we learn that we merely wanted them at a mental level. We want things with our minds, but we don't necessarily want things with our hearts. The mind is like an impatient child that makes continual demands and then forgets about them once it gets what it wants. It then soon becomes distracted with the next want. The mind is never satisfied, but if we get our hearts into what we want and feel what we want, we'll know that we truly want it beyond a compulsive mental level. The difference is that mental wanting is based in negativity, whereas heartfelt wanting is based in positivity. If the good feeling lasts well into attracting it, having it, and continually appreciating it, then we wanted it. We attract positive things into our lives because there is a sincere desire in our hearts to receive them. This is different from something that comes into our lives because a fleeting mental impulse gave us the compulsion to buy it. The things that we want with our hearts and feelings are what we truly want and truly allow.

We Block Ourselves

It may be challenging to spot these, but if we ask for something and find that our path becomes more difficult, it may be because we are trying to show ourselves that we need to release an internal blockage before we allow ourselves to have what we want. Something inside of us may be out of alignment with having or being what we want. If we are willing to be aware of and accept what arrives into our experience, we may find a link to why we won't allow ourselves to attract and have what we want.

For example, we may want something at the mental level, but our want could merely cover up a fear that is not aligned with our desire. Or maybe we have a fantastic dream, but our fear of making that dream a reality is greater than the desire to take steps to make it come true. All blockages will be negativity of some kind. Be mindful of this.

Ask yourself if there are any fears that you need to release to move forward and allow them to arrive into your awareness to be experienced, released and healed. Consider enlisting a consciously centered friend, minister or energy worker to assist you in taking steps to release the energetic blocks if you are ready to do so. During experiencing and releasing the fears and pains, remember why you are releasing them— because you want to allow more good things to come into your life. When we empty our cup of the things we do not want but give attention to, we can allow it to be filled with what we want to allow.

Mind Identified

When we are mind identified, we rely on mind impulses which we mistake for true heartfelt feelings. That's what I mean when I say that we feel with our minds and not our hearts. Do you think that we feel in our hearts that we want fast food several times each week? Our heart feelings don't want that. Our bodies don't want that, but the mind *does* want that fast food. Curious, isn't that? When we are mind-identified, we are stuck in mental wanting. These are ego impulses that promise lasting freedom but only deliver a short moment of relief until the next compulsive want arrives. This is a smokescreen, which prevents us from uncovering the real underlying issues that we may be afraid to release which aren't in alignment with what we are asking for. Succumbing to mind identification leads us into distraction after distraction, which prevents us from taking real steps in growth. Can you identify which distractions are preventing you from taking steps forward in your growth?

Lack

This is the big one. It can be challenging and elusive to understand the difference between creating from lack vs. creating from desire. When we're mentally identified—when we rely on mental impulses to get us through life without feeling from the heart—we usually experience what we want with a root feeling of lack behind our want. If we feel that we don't have something that we want, that want feeling comes from feeling like we don't have it, which is lack. The lack feeling is usually the underlying feeling doing the creating. Our minds say that we want it, but we feel that we don't have it.

We are confused about what desire is because we are creating from a place of lack. We think lack is desire because we feel strongly about our experience of displeasure. Life teaches us to push harder when this happens, but lack merely produces more lack. Desire means appreciating and feeling good about what we have and what we want to have. If we feel like we already have what we want, then we are feeling good inside. This feeling good inside, this feeling like we have what we want, is what desire truly is.

On the other hand, feeling like we don't have what we want is called lack. Trying to create from a feeling of not having, even when we say we want it, produces more of not having it. When we create from feeling good like we have it, or that we feel good because we know we will have it soon produces having it. Whether we use lack or desire to create, we are still creating, and the Law of Attraction is still working perfectly.

Understanding How Resistance Operates

Resistance can be a tricky thing, but it's also simple. Resistance is what covers up a fear that is not yet ready for release. When we feel resistance, it's good to choose a positive thought instead whenever we can. It's great if we can shift into positive thoughts and good feelings with relative ease. Yet, sometimes there is a need to express and release our resistance before we can access positive thoughts. If we need to release, it will feel good to release it by expressing it safely. It's never a good idea to suppress our resistance by burying it and turning it into passive aggression. When we do, we make the resistance more unconscious, and that is *not* what we want. Making things unconscious through avoidance and suppression gives unconsciousness more power, creates toxicity in the mind, invites illness and prevents us from moving forward in our development.

Healthy Release

Resistance can be expressed non-violently by talking with a consciously present friend, exercising, crying it out, screaming into a pillow. These forms of expression of resistance are beneficial when they make us feel better, feeling more balanced, relaxed, cleansed, relieved, peaceful or calm afterward.

Unhealthy Release

Expression of resistance will not be beneficial when it strengthens the resistance itself. Resistance (and stress) is suppressed fear. Resistance is any form of negativity, such as resentment, anger, irritation, annoyance, complaining, gossip, frustration, passive aggression, condescension, judgment. Indulging in any of these forms of negativity which leads to feeling tighter or more negative, is not releasing resistance; it's strengthening it.

By growing our conscious awareness and encouraging the healthy release of our resistance patterns, we can gain more alignment and turn our contraction into expansion.

The Law of Attraction

Wanting but Not Allowing

I think it's fascinating how my human ego-mind gives me all kinds of solutions that *it* thinks would make me happy, but in the end, that isn't true and lasting. I have before felt the need for change and the desire to make a change, but somehow I wouldn't *allow* the change to take place. So why do I do that?

For example, let's say that I want to own a horse, but I am afraid to ride one. What's going to happen there? I'm not going to be manifesting any horse, that's for sure. Let's look at it from another angle. What if I badly want a love relationship, but I am afraid of having my heart broken? What's going to happen there? No relationship. Or what if I would love to move to a new place to live and I have a list of healthy reasons why I would love to live there, but at the same time, I am afraid of losing the home that I live in now? What's going to happen there? No relocation.

The above are examples of why the Law of Attraction (LOA) doesn't *seem* to work for me. I've learned that when I believe that the LOA doesn't work, I am unaware that I am offering *opposing forces* in my energy. I say that I want things, but I might not understand how to align with my choices. So let's chat a bit about alignment.

Alignment Creates What We Want

Alignment means feeling good about who we are and where we are headed. Alignment is just feeling good. It doesn't matter what we're feeling good about. What so many of us don't understand about creating change is that when we are choosing to feel feelings of sadness, lack, fear, anger, resistance—even if we are feeling good about *some* things— the opposing forces result in us not allowing ourselves to have what we want. It is as if we are a train with two engines on each end, pulling us in opposite directions. The problem is that the opposing force creates no motion, except for a slow movement in the direction of the engine that pulls more strongly.

Why We Don't Manifest

We are motivated to create from the part of us that feels victimized. We tend to decide that it is time to manifest something we want because we're not feeling good. So, the impulse from which we decide we want more is the part of us that feels bad, victimized or powerless at that moment. When we're asking for what we want while feeling bad, we need to understand that these are the parts of us that believe that we can't feel better unless we have what we think we desperately need to feel better. So what do we naturally try to do from that standpoint? Force it. We push ourselves into creating what we want from the feelings of lack that we don't like! What's going to happen there? We're going to attract more frustration.

As evidenced by our negative feelings, our desire for change does not automatically mean that we require external change.

Instead, the true desire is to change something deep within us. This may be a limiting belief or conditioning that no longer serves us, manifesting as external conditions that no longer seem to fit us, but we may not be consciously aware of yet. Sometimes, the only way to know that we want change is by first experiencing what we don't want long enough to finally make a different conscious choice.

How We Can Manifest

There is no way to fool the God Source within us. Sure, we can create by pushing hard against resistance, which can still be successful. But creatorship need not be that hard. *If we allow ourselves to feel our God Source, then we can be in alignment with Source.* And guess what else? We'll then be in alignment with what we want.

The Secret Behind the Secret

Okay, here's the part that we rarely hear about the Law of Attraction. We don't want anything but God. It's true. *We don't want anything but God.* Why is this true? It's because anything that we desire to have must be accomplished through Him. (Sounds familiar, doesn't it?) "Through Him" means that when we are feeling good, we are feeling God. When we are feeling good, we are feeling the God within us that is real beyond illusion. *When we choose to direct our attention to things that make us feel good, we attract more feeling good.* We get into alignment.

Things start flowing into our experience. When we are not in alignment, things do not flow. We usually meet up with resistance when we are not flowing and forcing things instead.

What's the Catch?

"Why the hell are you doing this to me, God?" We all have done it. But there are a few things that the God Source within us is always guiding us to understand. So here are a few "catches" that I think God wants us to learn during our development here on earth and in using the Law of Attraction.

Catch #1: We *must* align with God to create anything of substance *because* all we want is God.

So why have desires if we don't want them, but we only want God? It's because our life path is *only* about our return to God. In this world of illusion, God has placed within us subtle reminders of what our return to Him means for us. These are our passions, desires and other things that feel good. Allowing these things to flow as we follow them attracts more of them to us. So all along, we are experiencing more of what we want because we are following what feels good and attracting more of the same. So we keep choosing to feel good, and our God Source rewards us because we are using our *willingness to choose* to connect with Him and what we want through Him. Why? Because *feeling good about* what we want equals *having* what we want. This is the whole premise behind these "think and grow wealthy" books, "using the subconscious power within you," "training your mind," "feeling your feelings." They're all tools that work according to the Law of Attraction, all of which are designed to promote alignment within us and, thus, align with God.

Catch #2: What feels good to us is for our alignment and not necessarily for others' alignments.

It is true that what is right for us as individuals is right for the whole of humanity. However, because we are all different expressions of God, each of our paths to God will differ. It is not our purpose to live exactly like everybody else does but rather live in a manner that feels good to us individually. By doing this, we trust the guidance God gives us. We will undoubtedly live a different life from others, and yet we can still be in alignment with God. We do this by feeling good about what we choose and what we have chosen.

What feels good to us is for our own alignment and development and does not necessarily apply to others because it is not their path. However, what does apply to others is that when we live our path in alignment with what feels good, we are helping others to do the same for themselves.

Other folks will have their path, and they will be spiritually attracted to other things. Choosing to focus on what feels good to us even if others do not feel good about the same things is spiritually honoring our guidance. This is different from others telling us what we "should" care about, which is always based on their fear, and probably a belief that they borrowed.

Spiritual development is highly specific to us as individuals. The feelings that we have are a natural and unique orientation that we each have that may not feel the same to others. This is why *practicing self-trust* is incredibly important on our spiritual paths. We can learn to follow those feelings in trust into the alignment the God Source in us wants to experience and know. Wouldn't it be nice if we learned how to listen to ourselves instead of taking people's word for things? The fact is that we do have all of the answers within us, and they are accessible by us.

Catch #3: Anything we quickly get bored with is not a real feeling.

The ego gets bored, not our God Source within. For example, impulse buying is mental (based on thinking), not spiritual (based on feeling). Many of us think we're feeling when we are merely negotiating with our mental impulses, unaware that we're disconnected from feelings and guidance. Through our minds alone, we give ourselves a temporary cessation, usually followed by the same cycle repeatedly. This is because, in our minds, we want comfort and familiarity more than we want true change. Any addiction would serve as an example. On the other hand, once we develop the courage and compassion for ourselves to honor our true feelings and not settle for familiarity when we want positive change, we will be guided when we want change the most. The draw to the peace of God is irresistible and irrefutable.

Countless minds want quick fixes to things only to be followed by more quick fixes. Quick-relief, quick, quick, quick! The ego-mind regards a detour as a nuisance and would like the familiarity reinstated immediately, but within these detours are the gifts that we give ourselves to get out of the mind. Hence, our boredom equals our temporary inability to recognize the gift that the present is giving us. The mind only wants a miracle when desperate for one, but we need to show the God within us some enduring willingness and true desire. Remember, we can't fool the God in us.

'How We Feel' Matters in Asking

Why don't more people want to act spiritual, you say? Well, everyone is spiritual by default. There's no way and nowhere but God. However, we do have the freedom to choose experiences that are not of God in this physical illusion, and we do choose them. The ability to choose helps us know which direction we want to go and if we want to return to God and, thus, return to ourselves. This means making a priority our choices to develop and feel things like self-love, self-acceptance, peace. The mind will overlook those lasting things that don't seem to yield instant gratification.

As long as I have the freedom to choose experiences not of God, I will have the option to experience the absence of God. Meaning, if I want to stay stuck, and choose fear and resistance instead of choosing what makes me feel better, then I wasn't willing to ask from a place other than fear or lack, and my mind got too bored to persevere.

Catch #4: If we're feeling good and feeling God, all things attract to us as we need them.

We can reverse the rules here and see that we are always provided for if we are always choosing to rest in God, meaning choosing to feel good, choosing to relax, choosing to follow the natural flow of our lives toward what thoughts and feelings feel better. This resting in God is the Holy Instant, where our willingness to accept things as they are aligns all things with us as needed. We don't have to hunt things down or mentally manage our lives. We begin to accept all people and all things as they are, and in creating this alignment through our acceptance, things naturally show

179

up for us as needed and without effort.

We Try to Manifest to Feel Better

How *could* we live our lives if we knew that all is provided for us if we align with our God Source Self within us? We might be more relaxed. We might trust more. We might feel better. *As we trust that we are provided for as we need things, our relaxed state won't cause us to ask for things we think we need to feel better. Instead, we'll just focus on feeling better!* As we continue to feel better, not only will we receive things, we may also ask for different things. This is because when we can provide the good feeling of God to ourselves, we don't feel the urge to ask for more, except to continue feeling God. So when all of our choices are in alignment with God, then what we want must come through because what we want is what God wants, not only for you or me but for the whole of humanity.

Forgiveness

Forgiveness

Forgiveness is Simple

As a wise friend once suggested, forgiveness is feeling with love what was once felt with fear. So let's talk about how we can get there.

Forgiveness itself is incredibly simple, yet it can be difficult to arrive at the point of readiness and allow it to happen. I will admit that forgiveness has been one of the last things that I have come to deeply understand for as long as I have studied and embraced personal growth. Why is that?

The undoing of the illusory mind is a lifelong process and an instant one, and for as many layers of the mind that we can peel away through our development, there are still more layers beyond that. The precept for our focus on this type of development is that the more illusion that we release within our mental and emotional bodies, the more we forgive and return to peace and well-being. We can reach these points of peace momentarily with our spiritual practices, yet I am speaking of the continued pursuit of reaching these places permanently. All of which reinforces our total self-acceptance.

Human Misconception

Like many spiritualists, I have gone above and beyond listening to my guidance, trusting myself more than anything or anyone else. The problem is that I have also misplaced my trust and protected my fears. This is not an awful, dark thing. It is a simple human misconception. Itis human nature to do the best with what we understand, and for what we do not understand, we improvise with our belief systems to help our minds function more completely day to day. I call this delicate dance of improvisation between our beliefs (substitutes for what we don't know) and our knowing (what we do know), Personal Truth and Universal Truth. The reason that we do this dance at all has to do with what we can "allow."

We have a relationship with our spirit within through which we enjoy, love and express life, and this mind of ours constantly tries to manage our spirit. Through our subconscious programming and the conscious compulsion to create and manage structure, the mind is (to a smaller or lesser degree) in constant competition with our spirit. So we are left constantly juggling between the mind and the spirit, doing the dance of feeling good and feeling bad as we cycle through our natural human and spiritual rhythms. Will we ever resolve their differences?

The Un-Surrendered Mind

The un-surrendered mind that competes with the free expression and feeling of the spirit can suppress our natural light. In doing so, the un-surrendered mind (also called ego) will create attachments to replace our trust in naturally surrendered living. We are taught to create these attachments because we are conditioned to believe that the world is unsafe. It can take us a lifetime to yield enough of these ego attachments to come to a place of surrendered living in our spiritual pursuit.

We have negative ego attachments: pain, suffering and unhealthy conditioning—the ego aspects that make us feel bad. We also have our positive ego attachments: accomplishment, identity and reputation—the ego aspects that make us feel good. The ego negatives make it easier for us to advance when we want to surrender because we know when we've had enough pain that we start praying, making new decisions. The ego positives are a bit trickier to release because a positive ego attachment gives us no incentive to release it. As long as we think we're doing a good job under any guise of ego, we won't see a need for any change. It isn't until we reach plateau after plateau that we find that roads walked in ego don't lead us anywhere real.

The Surrendered Mind

Our attachments of ego (the un-surrendered mind) are not "bad" in themselves. They are neutral. But if we surrender our minds, we become led by our spirit. This transforms the expression of our gifts into love and peace offerings and guides us to live from alignment instead of reinforcing the ego identity. It is up to us to live our lives each day and choose which place within we will come from, spirit or ego, surrendered mind or un-surrendered mind, love or fear.

Resolving the Conditioning

We have talked about how we practice spiritual living and how the ego-mind still interferes with us, seemingly blocking our way to God. So let's talk about what we can do to transcend our built-in blockage.

Remember, we are just as gifted with our ability to grow and develop as anyone else. We can heal ourselves and make ourselves feel better. Can you imagine what the world would look like if we could make ourselves feel better without having to go into the world expecting it to make us feel better? We would undoubtedly traverse many of the ego-mind's actions which teach us that we must build a defense against God. A "defense against God" means the actions we take based on non-trust, fear, and listening to needless hearsay over inner guidance. These defenses are all illusions that lead us ever more into the need for forgiveness.

Two overwhelming themes come to my mind regarding forgiveness as I learn about it and practice it. The first is that we don't know what forgiveness truly is, and the second is that it is not a priority to practice it.

We Don't Know Forgiveness

I'll bet you wonder how a defense against God would require something as seemingly unrelated as forgiveness. Forgiveness isn't only the traditional emotional release of pain, grievance, guilt or negativity towards self or others. Forgiveness is also the process by which our perceptions of illusion are healed as we are returned to God-consciousness. (See *A Course in Miracles*.)

We've been taught forgiveness as children. We've practiced it. Yet, we have little understanding of what forgiveness is. The concept of forgiveness seems to have become a mentally managed and conditioned faculty wherein little or nothing becomes transcended. In other words, there's no emotional release or change in perception. One reason why spiritual growth is so unpopular is that there is little incentive for the mind to undo itself. It's just the opposite. The mind prefers stimulation, not inactivity. The ego-mind naturally refuses the return to stillness and peace.

Mind Management

Mentally conditioned practices of anything do not guarantee that an energetic, emotional and transformative shift will occur in our feelings. What happens is that one mental program is instantaneously weighed against another with a quick evaluative comparison, including various components and circumstances, and whatever is deemed the most socially acceptable and least painful is chosen. This is clever mental management at best, not the undoing of illusion through forgiveness. The guise we are looking to resolve is the pre-programmed conditioning of the un-surrendered mind which, in time, tends to inhibit us from experiencing a real change in our feelings. Without this change in our feelings, forgiveness is meaningless.

How does programmed conditioning inhibit us? Well, have you noticed any suppressed people around? I have—including me! There is an entire world full of people who act one way but feel another. There are endless, countless emotions that aren't being felt or expressed, and they numb us into becoming inexpressive globs of carbon without our knowing it. Isn't it odd that we need to watch movies and television to experience that temporary lift that creates a change in our feelings? Our conditioning closes us off, prevents us from opening up to change, and if we don't watch it, the ego will continue to "Ease God Out" throughout our lives until all we feel like is a glob of carbon at the end.

We take so many outer, worldly steps and yet so few inner, emotional ones, and still, we compulsively wonder about the relationships we have with the world. We define success as something we do out in the world and not inside us, yet inside is where change matters most. Every material asset that we own seems to be an extension of what we have received because we pushed for it, and we weren't willing to give up. Does that last sentence make us feel proud or not?

The Priority of Forgiveness

It's not a priority to practice forgiveness because we feel things we may not want to feel. On top of that, when we do feel those things that surface, we don't feel good about them. We don't feel like they will go away. So the simple truth is that if we feel ugly things that feel like they won't go away, we try to avoid them. Our minds tell us to avoid whatever doesn't feel good.

What Forgiveness Is

Forgiveness is the choice to release ourselves from the prison of the un-surrendered ego-mind. Forgiveness means releasing pain, making emotional transitions, feeling better, going beyond the mind, and healing our errors in perception. Forgiveness bridges the gap between the surrendered mind and the un-surrendered mind. Forgiveness is the means through which we release our agenda and allow God's agenda to be completed through us.

Allowing - The Key to Forgiveness

The key to being able to forgive lies in "allowing" (or accepting). When we dissolve our mental resistance, we can feel and release unhealthy emotions. When we attempt to bury our emotions with the ego-mind's resistance, we may spend hours, days or longer engaging in short-lived or false feel-goods that mask how we feel and avoid addressing the emotions we don't want to feel. *The overlooked and important component of forgiveness is remembering that the feeling that doesn't feel good will dissolve if we allow it to be felt.* One way that forgiveness can be known is by feeling the emotions that need to be released. I consider prayer in asking God for assistance in this step to be crucial.

'The Serenity Prayer' works great. Once we have allowed ourselves to remove the resistance to our emotions, we are ready to feel our emotions. Sitting with our surrendered mind (no resisting) and emotions and allowing them to be felt will allow them to pass through us faster. If you are an expert crier who is great at cleansing, you know what I mean.

The Importance of Vigilance

When we ask God for help in self-forgiveness in creating positive change, it can be easy to forget that in our asking for help, it is always given. We don't always realize in our asking for forgiveness that we are immediately being given what we need. Sometimes we think our prayers are not being answered if we ask for guidance and then find ourselves being faced with feelings of resistance. But the gift that we give ourselves in those moments of receiving is the opportunity to address our blockage face to face. We are a perfect technology, and our vigilance must reflect our trust. We tell God, "God, I want such and such to happen internally or externally." Then the God within responds, "Okay, you asked for it! Here is the emotion or belief which you are holding onto and need to release and empty to fill up your cup again with what you want."

The ironic thing about asking for internal or external positive change is that it usually stems from feelings we think we *cannot* change. When we practice vigilance, however, we choose to remember that in asking for forgiveness of any kind, we are choosing to accept that whatever we are faced with is leading us directly into our process of forgiveness.

The Light of Presence

When we sit in the stillness of our surrendered minds without trying to change what we are feeling, we are "present." In our still presence, we are not reaching out into the future or past to change them. When we sit in still presence, we are no longer in conflict or resistance. This allows our emotional release to surface. As we do this, what is illusory in us is held up to the light to be felt, released, dissolved and cleansed. We may find that some emotions dissolve completely while others may require extra time to be worked through. Sometimes, a good cleansing cry is all we need to rebalance.

Whether emotions take seconds, days or months to release—
all of the process is normal.

The simplest and most potent spiritual practice of all time is
to *sit, feel and breathe through whatever you feel.*

How Transmutation Occurs

There is intelligence to the human being that is not managed
by the mind, although we think it is. There is a technology to
the body that knows how to balance itself if we allow it. A
simple experience of an emotion or feeling will change our
energetic alignment so profoundly so that we won't slip down
a conditioned pattern of mental resistance. Once the mind
has released its grip and our feelings have shifted or released
from within our bodies, we will begin to feel better. It may
not be immediately, but it can continue for hours in waves of
peace and feeling aligned and centered. In allowing this, we
have tapped into the intelligence of our Divine system,
working with it rather than against it. Any bit of allowing
ourselves to feel is acceptance and transcendence. No matter
what our ego-mind says to judge the feelings it does not want
to feel, accepting the feelings anyway will put us light years
ahead in our spiritual growth. Don't let the mind alone tell
you how spiritual you are; its assessment is vastly incorrect.

Asking For Magic

There is a difference between crying out of surrender and
healthy release versus crying out of pain. One cleanses us; the
other is resistance. Painful crying shows us that we are
intimately connected with what we want to change and can

set the stage for surrendering the mind and forgiving, but crying because of pain without releasing can go on indefinitely. We need to release, and when we can't, we ask for magic.

When we feel that we can't resolve things on our own, we are filled with prayer in the face of a challenge and forget that we created the challenge to release it and go free. However, that's rarely how we think of life. We think of challenges as having to "get around them" or "make the grade" or "just do enough to get by." We ask for magical circumstances, thinking that the world is troubling us when we create what we're getting.

Understanding Our Power

We are asking ourselves for guidance, and we are attracting the circumstances and people so that we can experience ourselves going through the fire of transmutation (forgiveness) and allowing the correction of the core error in our minds—the error that we aren't powerful. To think that we are going through a challenge to "get by" renounces all of our power as human beings. Getting by means that in our asking for healing, we remain unhealed. This viewpoint teaches us that we aren't who we truly are and that each choice we are faced with is not meant to change us for the better. It is meant to change us! We are meant to show up. Not only that, we are meant to show up as God would have us do so, and that means assuming that whatever is taking place is something that we've asked for. When we begin to discover that our asking for change truthfully denotes a redefinition in our power, we will begin to choose how we experience ourselves and our lives consciously.

Life Is Forgiveness

Asking for change masks what we are truly asking for underneath. The insight here is that we are always asking for forgiveness and self-acceptance. Our lives are a single process of asking for forgiveness and, more specifically, accepting ourselves. We merely go about reclaiming our forgiveness in varying degrees of time and effectiveness. We are always asking to feel better, but we don't know how to achieve feeling better, so we just ask for things and situations that help us feel better, and that does help. If we want to save time and skip a few steps, we can ask the God within to guide us into releasing what He would have us release to move forward into what we want with clarity, grace and greater acceptance of ourselves. Through working with God, we can combine our desire to forgive ourselves with the surrender that God leads us, transforming our lives into graceful and peaceful instruments of His Will.

Conclusion

Conclusion

Practicing Acceptance

From the trivial to the important, we can choose to practice acceptance with anything. Each effort makes a difference in our growth. It involves no one else knowing about it. The process is completely internal and occurs in our feelings. Our choice to practice acceptance helps us to accept not only others but also ourselves.

Worthiness

It is not necessary to become an expert at anything to feel self-acceptance or be a spiritual person. You are worthy no matter what, and you are lovable and deserve love. Being yourself and following the natural feel-good path in your life is as spiritual as you will ever need to be. So let the life you live touch others in the practice of what makes you feel acceptance, love, peace and joy for yourself.

Trusting Yourself

If you do have a desire to do or be something, then do it! Do it because it is in your heart to do it, not because anyone tells you that you should or shouldn't do it. Remember, your heart wants the experience; your ego demands the results. Your spiritual life expands from your experience, not from your bank statement. As with all things worthwhile, follow your heart. The greatest fulfillment in life comes from enjoying doing what is in your heart and forgetting about keeping score.

We don't need to walk the same path as other people walk unless it brings us joy. It brought me joy to write this book, but I do not expect anyone else to do the same thing. Our lives are our expression and experience, and by being brave enough to make our lives our own, we will expand and grow.

Expansion & Expression

Expressing who we are and how we feel is important. Whether we express to a friend, to God, on a canvas, through an instrument, by writing, by singing or some other way, energy must move through us for us to thrive. We are instruments of expansion. We practice acceptance not by suppressing how we feel but by expressing what we have within us to express.

Routine can provide stability and predictability, but too much of it for too long can inhibit the flow of energy through us. Doing the same old things *will* yield the same old results. Challenge yourself to do new things. Every choice for expansion counts, and the choice to express and expand is a practice of self-acceptance.

Understanding is Optional

We don't have to understand all of the details of life and how we internally operate to accept life as it is, enjoy it, allow it, and accept ourselves. The more we think, the more complexity we will discover. Conversely, the more we feel, the more freedom we will discover.

Teaching

If we are feeling acceptance, then we are teaching acceptance. Our teachers include not only those who offer us love but also those who trigger our non-acceptance. Accepting "button pushers" as our teachers will move us light years ahead in our spiritual growth. Sometimes, when we feel the most unspiritual by our usual standards, we have the greatest opportunity to learn and shine if we choose. Willingness is the key.

Being Open

It is far more powerful to have an open heart than a sharp mind. An open heart is the proof of an accepting mind. It is important to be open to other people's ideas and perspectives, no matter what we know. It is more important to enjoy the sharing and encouraging of ideas than it is to sell each other on ideas.

Accepting Love

We all want to be loved. We all want to be accepted. Underneath all of our attempts to gain acceptance from other people lies the desire to accept ourselves. No effort on our part is required to receive the love of God within us. We can learn to feel love and acceptance for ourselves without anyone's help but God's help. God loves each of us unconditionally.

We can share acceptance by giving a hug, volunteering our time or by just being there to support someone during a difficult time. We can do these things *right now* to feel love, peace and acceptance. We do not need to spend a lifetime proving to others or ourselves that we are lovable, successful, valuable or spiritual. At any time, we can be courageous and wise enough to give up the games that prevent us from feeling the love we are.

By allowing ourselves to feel and breathe through any emotion that arises within us, we are unconditionally loving and accepting ourselves. The more we do this, the more we realize our mastership as creators on this earth and open up to the kind of graceful living in acceptance that surpasses our wildest dreams.

Other books by the author:

Selling Emotionally Transformative Services: Business and
Self-Worth Advice Holistic Practitioners Need to Know

Selling Emotionally Transformative Services Companion
Notebook: Thought-Provoking Questions to Integrate and
Apply to Your Business

Butts in Seats: How to Get Clients and Launch Successfully
as a New Local Business

Made in the USA
Monee, IL
05 October 2021

79387609R00128